FantasyWorlds

Fantasy Worlds

Edited by Angelika Taschen

Idea and photographs by Deidi von Schaewen

Texts by John Maizels

TASCHEN

HONG KONG KÖLN LONDON LOS ANGELES MADRID PARIS TOKYO

© 2007 TASCHEN GmbH
Hohenzollernring 53, D-50672 Köln
www.taschen.com
Original edition: © 1999 Benedikt Taschen Verlag GmbH
© 2007 VG Bild-Kunst, Bonn, for the works by Niki de Saint Phalle,
Jean Tinguely and Ben Vautier
Edited by Angelika Taschen, Cologne
Designed by Armando Chitolina, Milan
Layout by Giorgio Martinoli, Milan
Texts edited by Ursula Fethke, Nazire Ergün, Viola Krauß, Cologne
Lithography by Horst Neuzner, Cologne
German translation by Susanne Helker, Cologne
French translation by Corinne Hewlett and Catherine Ianco, Paris
Cover design by Sense/Net, Andy Disl and Birgit Reber, Cologne

Printed in China
ISBN 978-3-8228-3219-6
ISBN 978-3-8228-3902-7 (edition with French cover)

Acknowledgements Danksagung
Remerciements

My greatest thanks go to all the artists and creators who have opened up their Fantasy Worlds to me on this long-drawn-out voyage and allowed me to take photographs of their inspiring creations. I hope that this will help to bring recognition of these marvelous environments and give more people a chance to see them.
I am greatly indebted to all the photographers, writers, publishers, film-makers and travellers whose books, magazines articles and films on this subject have for many years inspired me. It was they who implanted in me the desire to produce this book.
I am very grateful to Seymour Rosen from SPACES, to the Kohler Foundation, to Caroline Bourbonnais and many others, who helped in the battle to protect and restore certain of these environments. I should be very happy if this book were of assistance in that struggle and might stop the bulldozers (which recently struck again in Detroit).
On my many trips to all parts of the world I was given advice, encouragement and generous support by a large group of friends, colleagues and specialists. Their names have been listed by country. In France special thanks for abundant information to André Magnin and Jean Hubert Martin, also to Alexandra d'Arnoux, Paola Aragoni, Marie Odile and Antoine de Bary, Eva Bechmann, Eric Borja, François and Annie Chalin, Michèle Champenois, Melanie Chardayre, Yasha David, Laurent Danchin, Fabrice and Marcia Dubois la Chartre, Christian Duc, Gladys Fabre, Gaston, Philippe Issandon, Laurent Laidet, Nathalie du Luart, Irene Hutchinson, Christine and François Lippens, Paul and Françoise Maurer, Jean-Gabriel Mitterand, Renate Gallois Montbrun, Serge Peronnet, Anne and Patrick Poirier, Andrée Putman, Beatrice Rosenberg, Marie France Schneider, Ed Tuttle, Martine Valot and Jean Vircoulon.
In Germany many thanks to Dr. Albrecht Bangert, Ulf von Kanitz, Rixa von Treuenfels, Stefan Schomann, Alexander von Vegesack. In England, very special thanks to John Maizels and "Raw Vision" for his advice and directions; thanks also to Min Hogg, Lilianne Lijn, Charlotte Philipps and Richard Strange. In Switzerland particular thanks to Isa Hesse and Carol Roussopoulos. In Italy thanks to Barbara Rose. In America special thanks for their kind support to Seymour Rosen from SPACES, to Nancy H. Moulton from the Kohler Foundation, to Rebecca Hoffberger from the American Visionary Art Museum and to the Orange Show Foundation. Also warmest thanks to Sam and Laura Beizer, Peter Blake, Tom Johnston and Annie Friedmann, Pascal Galipean, Daniel Paul, Pam Strayer, Janet and Gerald Thomas, Sue Welsh, Ira Yeager and George. In Mexico all my thanks to Avery Danziger and Rosario Uranga. In India my gratitude to Patwant Singh, Meher Wiishaw and Rasil and Roman Basu. In Thailand, all my thanks to Pia Pierre and Carla. In South Africa particular thanks to Louise Hennigs and Hannes Myberg, also to Beezy Bailey, Jessica and John Clarke, Paul Gordon, Walter and Catharina Meyer, Gillian Rennie, Peter Rich, Jennifer Sorrell, and Jilly Stoltzman.
I am much indebted to Ursula Fethke and Nazire Ergün for their long and diligent coordination and their great editorial skills. Also my thanks to Armando Chitolina and Giorgio Martinoli for the very sensitive and beautiful layout; they are very diverse artists. And thanks to John Maizels for his informative and imaginative texts.

Paris, July 1999
Deidi von Schaewen

I would like to add my name to the grateful thanks to all those who have helped with the material for this book and especially to those whose research, writings, archives and published photographs have led the way in the appreciation of these wondrous places. Many thanks too to editors Ursula Fethke, Nazire Ergün and Chris Miller, and to our translators Susanne Helker, Corinne Hewlett and Catherine Ianco.

Letchmore Heath, July 1999
John Maizels

ContentsInhaltSommaire

Int
rodu
ct
ion

Einfü
hr
ung

FANTASY WORLDS *Introduction by John Maizels* In the late 1870s, a country postman in France stumbles on a strangely shaped stone. Fascinated, he picks it up and feels urged to collect others. Before too long he has amassed hundreds and begins to form them into a construction. Thirty three years later the immense and extraordinary Palais idéal (see 94–97) near Lyon nears completion.

In Chandigarh, Northern India, in the Sixties, a roads inspector becomes obsessed with the spirits he believes lie within the rocks and stones he collects together in a forest clearing. Before too long he builds them into walls and courtyards, figures and beasts. Over 30 years later The Rock Garden of Chandigarh (see pages 212–217) contains 25 acres of countless hundreds of statues, waterfalls, buildings and walkways.

What is the link between these events? How is it that from such humble and unplanned beginnings such ambitious and overpowering creations can ensue? The urge to decorate and embellish one's dwelling is a common and primal force, even evident in the animal kingdom. For some people, though, it becomes an obsession, far outstretching the simple shell-embellished sea-side porch, or the witty garden gazebo. For some, a hobby or a digression develops into a life's work, a quest to leave a unique and undeniable mark on the world which reflects their own inner vision. An attempt to create a genuine alternative reality for themselves, their very own earthly paradise.

This book collects together 62 of the most extreme and extraordinary examples of environmental creations that have dominated the lives of their creators over decades. It is the result of more than twenty years of travel by photographer Deidi von Schaewen who has made her own documentation of these sites from the United States, from Europe, from Asia and Africa. These phenomena have

FANTASY WORLDS *Einleitung von John Maizels* In den späten siebziger Jahren des 19. Jahrhunderts stolperte ein Briefträger in Frankreich über einen ungewöhnlich geformten Stein. Er war augenblicklich von ihm fasziniert und begann, weitere zu sammeln. Nach kurzer Zeit war seine Sammlung auf Hunderte von Steinen angewachsen, und Ferdinand Cheval nahm die Errichtung seines monumentalen und ungewöhnlichen Palais idéal bei Lyon in Angriff, den er 33 Jahre später fertigstellte. In den sechziger Jahren sammelte ein Straßenbauinspektor im nordindischen Chandigarh aus religiöser Überzeugung Steine und Felsen. Er arrangierte die nach seinem Glauben beseelten Fundobjekte auf einer Lichtung im Dschungel zu Mauern, Höfen, Figuren und Tieren. In einem Zeitraum von mehr als 30 Jahren schuf Nek Chand auf einem Areal von 10 Hektar Land den Rock Garden of Chandigarh (siehe Seite 212–217) mit zahllosen Statuen, Wasserfällen, Gebäuden und Gehwegen.

Was haben diese Ereignisse gemeinsam? Welche Energie trieb die Künstler an, die aus einer spontanen Idee heraus diese großartigen, ehrgeizigen Werke schufen? Es ist ein natürliches Bedürfnis von Menschen, aber auch Tieren, die eigene Umwelt zu gestalten und zu verschönern. Bei einigen Menschen entsteht daraus eine Obsession, die bei weitem über den Wunsch hinausgeht, eine Veranda mit Meerblick mit Muscheln zu dekorieren oder witzige Pavillons in den Garten zu stellen. Für einige wird das Hobby oder der Zeitvertreib zur Lebensaufgabe, zu dem Bedürfnis, ein einzigartiges Zeugnis zu hinterlassen, das ihre persönliche Vision widerspiegelt – der Versuch, eine alternative Realität zu schaffen, ihr ganz eigenes

MONDES IMAGINAIRES *Introduction de John Maizels* Au siècle dernier, à la fin des années soixante-dix, un facteur en France butte sur un caillou aux formes étranges. Il le ramasse et, fasciné, commence à en récolter d'autres. Bien vite, il en amasse des centaines et entreprend de les assembler. Trente-trois plus tard, l'extraordinaire Palais idéal (voir pages 94–97) près de Lyon est presque achevé. Plus près de nous, dans les années soixante, un inspecteur de la voirie de Chandigarh, au nord de l'Inde, accumule dans une clairière des pierres qui, pour lui, abritent des esprits. Puis il construit avec ces roches des murs, des bâtiments, des personnages, des animaux. Plus de 30 ans plus tard, le Jardin de pierre de Chandigarh (voir pages 212–217) de douze hectares mêle statues, édifices, chemins et cascades.

Qu'est-ce qui réunit ces deux entreprises? Comment des débuts si modestes, dus au hasard, ont-ils donné naissance à des réalisations aussi grandioses que captivantes? Le besoin de décorer et d'embellir son habitat est une impulsion puissante, commune à bien des êtres, y compris dans le règne animal. Pour certaines personnes, elle se transforme en une véritable obsession qui dépasse de loin l'aménagement d'un petit kiosque au fond du jardin ou d'un portail décoré de coquillages pour une villa balnéaire. Ce qui n'était au départ qu'un passe-temps ou une parenthèse finit par occuper une vie entière, par devenir une tentative d'inscrire dans le monde une marque durable et très personnelle, une réalité alternative, un

The Garden of Palazzo Orsini,
Bomarzo, Italy.

paradis individuel. Qualifiés aujourd'hui d'«environnements visionnaires», ces sites sont souvent l'œuvre de gens avec peu ou pas de formation artistique, poussés par une vision et un élan créateur dont la force ne cesse de croître avec le temps.

Cet ouvrage présente 62 environnements visionnaires extrêmes qui ont occupé leurs créateurs pendant des dizaines d'années. Il est le résultat d'un travail de plus de vingt ans mené par la photographe Deidi von Schaewen qui, au cours de ses voyages, a constitué un fonds considérable sur des sites d'Amérique, d'Europe, d'Asie et d'Afrique.

Ni Ferdinand Cheval (1836–1924), créateur du Palais idéal, ni Nek Chand Saini (*1924), bâtisseur du Jardin de pierres de Chandigarh, le plus grand environnement visionnaire au monde, n'imaginaient les proportions qu'allait prendre leur projet. Parmi les sites de ces artistes singuliers, bien peu sont nés d'une conception d'ensemble. Raymond Isidore (1904–1964), dit Picassiette, a commencé par couvrir des pots de fleurs de mosaïques en vaisselle cassée; puis il a incrusté de tessons l'intérieur et l'extérieur de sa petite maison (voir pages 80–83) à Chartres, avant de procéder de même dans sa cour et son jardin. Il a finalement consacré presque 30 ans à son œuvre. Simon Rodia (1875–1965) savait seulement qu'il voulait faire «quelque chose de grand»: ses gigantesques Tours de Watts (voir pages 200–207), à Los Angeles, incarnent 33 ans de labeur titanesque.

Visionnaires travaillant pour eux-mêmes, à l'écart du milieu de l'«art culturel» auquel aucune formation ne les a initiés, ces créateurs sont aujourd'hui fermement inscrits dans la catégorie de l'«art brut». La notion a été théorisée par l'artiste Jean Dubuffet (1901–1985). Ce dernier s'est inspiré des études du docteur Hans Prinzhorn et d'autres psychiatres éclairés qui avaient su reconnaître la valeur intrinsèque d'œuvres produites par des aliénés, et qui ne considéraient pas l'art comme le domaine réservé de praticiens formés par des études et disposant de vastes connaissances. Dubuffet a compris que toutes sortes de créateurs solitaires dotés d'une personnalité affirmée peuvent élaborer en dehors des normes culturelles des œuvres fortes, uniques. Il ne s'agit pas seulement de malades mentaux. La création véritable surgit aussi

aradies auf Erden. Das Buch stellt 62 der bemerkenswertesten Beispiele von sogenannten Visionary Environments vor, die von Künstlern über Jahrzehnte hinweg errichtet wurden. Im Lauf einer mehr als zwanzigjährigen Recherchearbeit hat die Fotografin Deidi von Schaewen die interessantesten Werke in den Vereinigten Staaten, Europa, Asien und Afrika ausführlich dokumentiert. Ihre Erbauer verfügten oft über nur über geringe oder sogar gar keine künstlerische Ausbildung, sondern vertrauten auf ihre persönliche Vision und Kreativität, deren Intensität mit den Jahren wuchs.

Die wenigsten Künstler hatten zu Beginn ihrer Arbeit ein ehrgeiziges Ziel. Als der französische Postbote Ferdinand Cheval (1836–1924) mit der Arbeit an seinem Palais idéal begann, ließ er sich nicht träumen, daß dieser ihn noch in den folgenden 33 Jahren beschäftigen würde. Genauso ging es Nek Chand Saini (*1924) aus Chandigarh, dem Erbauer des weltweit größten und wohl bemerkenswertesten Visionary Environment, als er versuchsweise seine ersten Gestalten aus Steinen und Altmaterialien formte. Raymond Isidore (1904–1964), der unter dem Künstlernamen Picassiette bekannt wurde, stellte zunächst Blumentöpfe her, die er mit Mosaiken aus zerbrochenem Geschirr verzierte. Anschließend bedeckte er die Außen- und Innenwände seines kleinen Hauses (siehe Seite 80–83) in Chartres mit Mosaiken und ließ seiner Kreativität dann im Hof und im Garten freien Lauf. Auch Picassiette investierte fast 30 Jahre Arbeit in seine Schöpfung. Simon Rodia (1875–1965) behauptete, er habe nur das vage Gefühl gehabt, »etwas Großes« schaffen zu müssen. Auch seine gigantischen Watts Towers (siehe Seite 200–207) in Los Angeles waren das Ergebnis von 33 Jahren Arbeit.

Diese Künstler lassen sich im allgemeinen der »Outsider Art« oder auch »Art Brut« zuordnen. Sie handeln als Visionäre, ohne Ausbildung und mit wenig oder gar keiner Verbindung zur konventionellen Kunstwelt. Die Bezeichnung »Art Brut« wurde erstmals von dem französischen Künstler Jean Dubuffet (1901–1985) verwendet. Dubuffet war von den Entdeckungen von Hans Prinzhorn und anderer hellsichtiger Psychiater beeinflußt worden. Sie hatten erkannt, daß manche der Arbeiten psychiatrischer Patienten außergewöhnliche Qualitäten besaßen und daß der Begriff »Kunst« nicht allein auf die Werke ausgebildeter Künstler oder den Kreis kultivierter Personen beschränkt werden konnte. Dubuffet stellte fest, daß diese idiosynkratischen und äußerst individualistischen Persönlichkeiten eine ganze Bandbreite einzigartiger und kraftvoller Ausdrucksformen fanden, und zwar völlig auf sich

become known as "visionary environments". They are in the main created by those with little or no formal art education, who find themselves being driven by a vision and a creative force that increases in intensity over the years.

Few of these places have been initiated with the ambitious end result in mind. The French postman Ferdinand Cheval (1836–1924), creator of the Palais idéal, slowly began his momentous construction, not knowing that it would occupy him for the next 33 years. Similarly Nek Chand Saini (*1924), in Chandigarh, creator of the World's largest and most spectacular visionary environment, tentatively began to take his first steps in creating his own forms from stones and waste materials. Raymond Isidore (1904–1964), known as "Picassiette", began by making flower pots covered with a mosaic of broken plates and then went on to encrust both the outside and interior of his small house (see pages 80–83) in Chartres before spreading his creative force around the courtyards and garden of his property, again spending almost 30 years on his creation. Simon Rodia (1875–1965) claims that he just had a notion to do "something big" and once more, his giant Towers (see pages 200–207) in Watts, Los Angeles, were the result of 33 years of epic toil.

These artists now find themselves firmly within the category of "outsider art" or "art brut", the work of untrained visionaries who work only for themselves, with little or no connection with the art world. The theory of "art brut" was first formulated by French artist Jean Dubuffet (1901–1985). He was in turn inspired by the discoveries of Dr Hans Prinzhorn and other enlightened psychiatrists who came to the realisation that some of the artworks produced by inmates of mental institutions were extraordinary in their own right, that art was not solely the preserve of trained practitioners and high culture. Dubuffet saw that unique and powerful art, completely uninfluenced by cultural norms, could be produced by a whole range of idiosyncratic

and strongly individual creators operating entirely on their own. This was not just the work of the mentally ill or unstable but a source of true creation, carried out as the result of inner compulsion. An art as natural and free-flowing as a child's, but with the full intensity, sophistication and commitment of an adult. From the mid Forties, Dubuffet began to seek out and collect such works, which he termed "art brut": raw art. "Raw" because it was uncooked by culture. "Raw" because it was a link to the raw nerve of the psyche. His great collection was opened to the public in 1976 in a purpose-built museum, the Musée de l'Art Brut in Lausanne. In addition to the two and three dimensional works in his huge collection, Dubuffet acknowledged the environmental creations of similar artists. Although Dubuffet, and the surrealists too, were familiar with the Palais idéal and a few other such places, it is only since the Seventies that many of these creations have come to light. Unlike many of the socially and culturally isolated artists in Dubuffet's collection, the environmental creators are usually solid, if eccentric, members of their local communities. Many have had to create in their spare time after a regular days work, others started their creations after retirement. Others in this book fall more into the category of the visionary sophisticate; professional architects or artists who have indulged their personal vision to create their fantasies. These are often more planned affairs, but have a close affinity to the works of the purely intuitive self-taught creators of outsider art. For these quirky architects one can find historical antecedents in the follies, grottos and hermitages of the 17th century onwards. Garden building and ornament on a large

Giovanni Battista Piranesi,
The Drawbridge
Die Zugbrücke
Le Pont-levis,
Carceri d'Invenzione (1761)

gestellt und unbeeinflußt von kulturellen Normen. Diese Werke waren für Dubuffet mehr als der Ausdruck psychisch kranker oder labiler Menschen. Sie sind das Ergebnis eines inneren, fast zwanghaften Bestrebens, das eine natürliche und frei fließende Arbeitsweise, fast kindliche Naivität sowie die Intensität, das Wissen und das Engagement des Erwachsenen miteinander verbindet.

Dubuffet begann Mitte der vierziger Jahre, »Art-Brut«-Werke zu suchen und zu sammeln. »Art Brut« (rohe Kunst) wurde sie deshalb genannt, weil sie nicht »in Kultur durchgekocht« worden war und weil sie die innere Vision der Künstler ohne rationale Einschränkungen darstellte. Im Jahr 1976 wurde das Musée de l'Art Brut in Lausanne eröffnet, das Dubuffets umfangreiche Sammlung der Öffentlichkeit zugänglich machte. Neben den zwei- und dreidimensionalen Werken seiner Sammlung erkannte Dubuffet auch die Visionary Environments als Ausdruck dieser Kunstrichtung an. Obwohl er und auch die Surrealisten den Palais idéal sowie einige wenige andere Projekte kannten, vollzog sich die eigentliche Entdeckung der meisten Environments erst in den siebziger Jahren.

Im Gegensatz zu den vielen sozial und kulturell isolierten Künstlern, deren Werke zu Dubuffets Sammlung gehören, sind die Schöpfer der Visionary Environments in der Regel gut in ihre örtlichen Gemeinschaften integriert, auch wenn sie oft als Exzentriker angesehen werden. Meistens haben sie eine feste Arbeitsstelle und widmen sich ihren Werken in der Freizeit oder erst während der Rente.

Weitere, in diesem Buch vorgestellte Künstler fallen in die Kategorie der »gebildeten Visionäre«: ausgebildete Künstler oder Architekten, die ihrer persönlichen Vision freien Lauf ließen und eine Phantasiewelt schufen. Projekte dieser Art wurden meist sorgfältig geplant, zeichnen sich aber dennoch durch eine Affinität zu den Werken der Outsider-Künstler aus, die sich allein von ihrer Intuition leiten lassen. Für ihre eigenwilligen Schöpfungen finden sich historische Vorläufer in den Zierbauten, Grotten und Einsiedeleien, wie sie seit dem 17. Jahrhundert errichtet wurden. Gartenarchitektur und die Dekoration ganzer Gartenanlagen in großem Stil begann im 16. Jahrhundert in Italien und verbreitete sich von dort aus allmählich über ganz Europa, gleichzeitig mit der Idee, daß der Garten selbst bis ins kleinste Detail gestaltet werden sollte. In den

d'êtres mus par un élan intérieur, aussi naturelle et libre que celle d'un enfant mais intense, complexe et engagée comme celle d'un adulte.

Au milieu des années quarante, Dubuffet commence à collectionner de l'«art brut», ainsi qu'il le nomme: brut parce qu'il n'a pas été transformé par la culture, brut parce qu'il procède des zones sensibles du psychisme. Sa collection immense de pièces en deux et trois dimensions est ouverte au public en 1976, dans le Musée de l'Art brut à Lausanne. Dubuffet, comme les surréalistes, connaît le Palais idéal du facteur Cheval et quelques autres environnements visionnaires, qu'il apprécie à leur juste valeur. Toutefois, ce n'est que dans les années soixante-dix que ces sites commencent à être reconnus.

A l'inverse des artistes de la collection Dubuffet qui se situent aux marges de la culture et de la société, les créateurs d'environnements visionnaires sont généralement bien intégrés, même s'ils font figure d'excentriques. Bon nombre ont un emploi et créent pendant leurs loisirs, d'autres entreprennent leur travail une fois à la retraite.

Certains ensembles présentés dans l'ouvrage relèvent d'une catégorie plus sophistiquée: ils sont le fait d'architectes ou d'artistes professionnels qui ont donné libre cours à leur fantaisie, à leurs visions personnelles. Ces projets plus programmés ont cependant une affinité étroite avec les œuvres d'autodidactes guidés par leur seule intuition. Ils ont pour ancêtres les grottes, les folies et les ermitages en vogue à partir du 17e siècle. Les grottes elles-mêmes s'inspirent des lieux de culte grecs d'avant les temples, des autels domestiques des Romains, du caveau où fut déposé le corps du Christ, autant de refuges sacrés, imprégnés de mystère. L'architecture des jardins, la décoration à grande échelle de parcs entiers, apparaît au 16e siècle en Italie. Elle se répand dans toute l'Europe, en même temps que l'idée d'un jardin qu'il faudrait modeler dans ses moindres détails. L'étrange parc de Bomarzo, en Italie, construit par Pirro Ligorio pour Pier Francesco Orsini, duc de Bomarzo (environ 1513–1584),

Photo: Scala

Giambologna,
The Appennino Statue
and Fountain,
Villa Demidoff,
Pratolino, Italy

scale originated in 16th-century Italy and gradually spread to the rest Europe along with the concept of garden design itself. The bizarre gardens at Bomarzo, Italy, built by Pirro Ligorio for Pier Francesco Orsini, Duke of Bomarzo (c. 1513–1584), included a giant mouth as an entrance and a Leaning House built at an angle. The gardens at the Villa Pratolino near Florence contained a grotto fronted by a huge figure of Appennino by Giambologna (1529–1608). The fashionable gardens of European aristocracy began to sport all manor of sham ruins and architectural pastiche, but some included original designs for arbours, grottos and hermitages. Grotto building in Europe continued the tradition of constructing shrines along pilgrim routes or at sacred places and developed into an indigenous folk art that from time to time resurfaces in the work of intuitive builders even today. The highly elaborate architectural fantasies of the Venetian artist Giambattista Piranesi (1720–1778) typify the fascination for elaborate forms which had their root in classical antiquity. In his series of etchings of the "Carceri", Piranesi used classical elements to visualise huge internal structures of endless arches and columns. By this time the fashion for grottos had spread to fashionable and wealthy houses, with "grotto rooms", covered in shells and stones, being a common feature of many grand homes, as well as free standing structures carefully placed in expansive gardens. Wilhelmine, the Margavine of Bayreuth, (1709–1758), transformed a simple hunting lodge into a highly idiosyncratic "Hermitage", starting in 1735. A subterranean passage leads to the grotto room, which was densely ornamented with glass, slag and shells and included the fantasy figures of marine beasts. It also contained 200 water jets that could drench unsuspecting guests, much to the amusement of members of the court.

Gärten von Bomarzo in Italien, die Pirro Ligorio für den Grafen von Bomarzo, Pier Francesco Orsini (um 1513–1584), entwarf, stehen ein »schiefes Haus« und ein riesiges Maul, das als Tor dient. In den Gärten der Villa Pratolino bei Florenz wacht die große Skulptur des Apennin von Giambologna (1529–1608) über den Eingang einer Grotto. Verschiedenste »Ruinen« und Architekturpastichen waren damals in den Gärten der europäischen Aristokratie in Mode, aber auch Lauben, Grotten und Einsiedeleien. Die Tradition der Grotte läßt sich in Europa zurückführen auf die Kapellen, die entlang der Pilgerwege oder an heiligen Orten errichtet wurden. Daraus entstand eine regelrechte Volkskunst, die auch heute noch von Zeit zur Zeit hervortritt in den Werken von intuitiv und spontan handelnden Künstlern.

Die höchst kunstvollen Architekturphantasien des venezianischen Künstlers Giambattista Piranesi (1720–1778) belegen die Faszination, die die hochentwickelte Architektur der Antike ausstrahlte, zum Beispiel in den »Invenzioni di Carceri«, wo Piranesi klassische Architekturelemente für die Innenansichten von riesigen Hallen mit endlosen Bogen- und Säulenreihen verwendete. Zu diesem Zeitpunkt hatte die »Grottenmode« die Häuser der Reichen und Kultivierten erreicht: Jedes vornehme Haus verfügte über eine Grotte, entweder als integrierter Raum, der mit Muscheln und Steinen verziert war, oder als freistehendes Gebäude in einem weitläufigen Park.

Ab 1735 verwandelte die Markgräfin Wilhelmine von Bayreuth (1709–1758) eine einfache Jagdhütte in eine eigenwillige Einsiedelei. Sie bestand aus einer durch einen unterirdischen Gang erreichbare Grotte, die mit Meeresungeheuern sowie über und über mit Glas, Schlacke und Muscheln geschmückt war. Zum Vergnügen des Hofes konnten die überraschten Gäste mit Wasser aus 200 Fontänen besprizt werden.

Ein herausragendes Beispiel für eine freistehende Grotte ist Ascot House in Berkshire in England, das vermutlich im Auftrag des Besitzers ab 1740 errichtet wurde und dessen Räume und Bassins mit Stalaktiten und Steinen geschmückt sind. Zeitgenössische Musterbücher für Architekten zeigen auch Entwürfe für Einsiedeleien, die als rohgezimmerte Unterstände dem Besitz einen pittoresken Zug verliehen. Einer der großen englischen Erbauer von solchen Gebäuden war Thomas Wright, dessen Einsiedelei Hermit's Cave in Badminton nach 250 Jahre immer noch steht. Sie wurde aus großen Wurzeln und knotigen Ästen errichtet und ist ein wunderbares Beispiel für Zierbauten dieser Art. Wrights Buch »Universal Architecture« (1755) enthält eine ganze Reihe von Entwürfen für eigenwillige Gebäude in Gartenanlagen.

comportait une tour penchée bâtie de guingois et un portail d'entrée en forme de gueule béante. Près de Florence, les jardins de la villa de Pratolino abritaient une grotte surmontée d'une énorme statue de dieu figurant l'Apennin, réalisée par Giambologna (1529–1608). Les jardins à la mode de l'aristocratie européenne s'ornèrent de toutes sortes de fausses ruines et de pastiches architecturaux et, pour certains, de charmilles, de grottes et de retraites tout à fait originales. Dans la tradition des chapelles construites le long des routes de pélerinage et sur des sites sacrés, les grottes donnèrent aussi naissance à un art populaire qui se manifeste encore parfois dans les œuvres des bâtisseurs visionnaires de notre temps.

Les fantaisies architecturales très recherchées de l'artiste vénitien Piranèse (1720–1778) trahissent la fascination exercée par des formes élaborées inspirées de l'antiquité classique. Dans ses vues de prisons (Invenzioni di Carceri), Piranèse utilise des éléments classiques pour concevoir d'énormes salles, animées de colonnes et d'arcades sans fin. A son époque, la mode des grottes s'était étendue aux demeures aisées: des pièces aux murs incrustés de coquillages et de pierres ornaient bon nombre de maisons somptueuses ou se dressaient dans leurs parcs, à des emplacements choisis avec soin. A partir de 1735, Wilhelmine, margrave de Bayreuth (1709–1758), entreprit de transformer un simple pavillon de chasse en un étonnant «ermitage». Un passage souterrain menait à la grotte, richement décorée de verre, de scories volcaniques et de coquillages, et peuplée de monstres marins. Deux cents jets d'eau aspergeaient les visiteurs non avertis, au plus grand amusement de la cour. En Angleterre, on trouve à Ascot House, dans le Berkshire, un exemple particulièrement remarquable de grotte bâtie de toutes pièces, datant des années 1740; elle fut construite, semble-t-il, sur décision du propriétaire et comporte plusieurs salles et bassins décorés de stalactites et

The Pineapple House, Dunmore Park, Stirlingshire, Scotland (1761)

Christian Jank,
Sketch for a castle on the Falkenstein for Ludwig II of Bavaria.
Entwurf für eine Burg auf dem Falkenstein für Ludwig II.
Projet d'un château fort sur le Falkenstein pour Louis II de Bavière.

One outstanding example still in existence in England of a free-standing grotto is at Ascot House, Berkshire, apparently built on the owner's instructions in the 1740s and containing several chambers and pools and encrusted with stalactites and minerals. Builder's pattern books of the time also contained designs for hermitages, roughly made wooden shelters to adorn some picturesque spot on an estate. One great English folly builder was Thomas Wright, whose Hermit's Cave at Badminton, still in existence after 250 years, was constructed of giant roots and gnarled branches, and typified the style of the genre. His book "Universal Architecture" (1755) contained a whole range of quirky designs for garden buildings. A great many follies of the 18th century were substantial buildings; one of the more unusual being The Pineapple House in Sterlingshire, Scotland, built for the Earl of Dunmore in 1761, to glorify his horticultural achievements. In other parts of Europe such creations as the villa of the Prince of Pallagonia near Palermo and the extravagant fairy tale castle of "mad" King Ludwig II of Bavaria (1845–1886), at Neuschwanstein, further developed the tradition of highly inventive architecture constructed on the orders of an eccentric patron.

In more modern times one can look to the extraordinary genius of Antoni Gaudí (1852–1926). Supported by wealthy sponsors, especially by his friend Eusebi Güell, he was a rare example of an architect able to let his fertile imagination combine with innovative architectural technique. From his first commission, the Casa Vicens which he began in 1883, Gaudí began to evolve his organic method of working, where one thing would lead to another without total adherence to a preconceived plan. From the beginning he used a mixture of ceramic tile and cheap stone and rubble to decorate his surfaces. It was Güell who commissioned Gaudí to create a new park in Barcelona which allowed him the freedom to reach the full maturity of his style, culminating in the endlessly flowing bench on the terrace, richly ornamented with colourful broken ceramic. In the same period he constructed the Casa Batlló (1904–1906), a flowing organic structure that seems to be more a sculpture than a building.

Archiv für Kunst und Geschichte, Berlin

Sehr viele der Ziergebäude des 18. Jahrhunderts waren richtige Häuser, wie zum Beispiel das ungewöhnliche Pineapple House (Ananashaus) in Sterlingshire in Schottland, das 1761 für den Earl von Dunmore in Anerkennung seiner gärtnerischen Verdienste errichtet wurde. Schöpfungen wie die Villa des Prinzen von Pallagonien bei Palermo und das extravagante Märchenschloß Neuschwanstein, das für den »verrückten« König Ludwig II. von Bayern (1845–1886) erbaut wurde, setzten die Tradition einer höchst erfindungsreichen Architektur im Auftrag exzentrischer Persönlichkeiten fort.

Heute kann man in Barcelona das Werk des genialen Antoni Gaudí (1852–1926) bewundern, der von reichen Geldgebern und vor allem von seinem Freund Eusebi Güell unterstützt wurde. Gaudí gehört zu den wenigen Architekten, die reiche Phantasie und innovativen technischen Geist miteinander verbanden. Bei seiner ersten Auftragsarbeit, der Casa Vicens, die ab 1883 errichtet wurde, begann Gaudí, nach einer Arbeitsmethode zu arbeiten, bei der sich der Bau – ohne völlig einem vorher erdachten Plan zu folgen – organisch von selbst entwickelt. Als Dekor wählte er von Anfang an eine Mischung aus Keramikkacheln sowie preiswertem Stein und Schutt. Als Güell Gaudí damit beauftragte, einen neuen Park in Barcelona zu schaffen, konnte dieser seinen Stil zur vollen Reife entwickeln. Gaudís Eigenart zeigt sich zum Beispiel im Park Güell bei der Bank mit den fließenden Formen, die mit farbenfrohen Keramikscherben verziert ist. Zur selben Zeit errichtete Gaudí die Casa Batlló, deren organisch fließende Formen eher einer Skulptur als einem Haus gleichen. Gaudís Lebenswerk wurde die Sagrada Familia, die durch eine öffentliche Ausschreibung finanziert wurde und der er sich ab 1914 ausschließlich widmete. Die Kirche ist heute noch unvollendet und legt Zeugnis ab für den Genius eines höchst individuellen Architekten. Auch der österreichische Künstler Friedensreich Hundertwasser (1928–2000) hat phantasievolle und individualistische Werke geschaffen. Nur einige wenige seiner revolutionären Gebäude- und Stadtentwürfe sind ausgeführt worden, darunter Wohnhäuser und Kirchen wie das Hundertwasser-Haus in Wien und die St. Barbara-Kirche in Bärnbach in der Steiermark.

de roches. A l'époque, les manuels et livres de croquis à l'usage des bâtisseurs proposaient des modèles d'ermitages, abris grossiers en bois destinés à compléter un point de vue pittoresque dans un parc. On doit à Thomas Wright, grand constructeur de folies, la Hermit's Cave de Badminton, conservée jusqu'à nos jours. Fabriquée à partir de racines et de branches noueuses, c'est un parfait exemple du genre. L'ouvrage de Wright intitulé «Universal Architecture» (1755) présentait toute une gamme de croquis originaux pour des architectures de jardin.

Quantité de folies du 18e siècle étaient en fait de véritables édifices. Parmi les plus étonnants, citons la Pineapple House (la Maison de l'ananas) dans le Sterlingshire, en Ecosse, élevée à la gloire des réussites horticoles du comte de Dunmore, en 1761. Ailleurs en Europe, des réalisations telles que la villa du prince de Pallagonia, près de Palerme, ou le château fantastique de Louis II de Bavière (1845–1886), à Neuschwanstein, vinrent enrichir la longue lignée de ces édifices inventifs voulus par des commanditaires excentriques.

Plus près de nous, on évoquera le génie d'Antonio Gaudí (1852–1926) qui a laissé ses traces à Barcelone. Aidé par de riches mécènes, au premier rang desquels son ami Eusebio Güell, il fournit l'exemple rare d'un architecte qui a su marier une imagination fertile et des techniques architecturales innovatrices. Dès sa première commande, la Casa Vicens en 1883, Gaudí commence à mettre au point sa méthode organique, où une chose mène à la suivante sans souci d'un plan préétabli. Il adopte immédiatement pour la décoration des surfaces un mélange de carreaux de céramique, de pierres communes et de matériaux divers. C'est également Güell qui commande à Gaudí un nouveau parc dans Barcelone, travail grâce auquel le style de l'architecte atteint sa pleine maturité. On en veut pour preuve le banc qui

Gaudí's life work became the Cathedral of the Sagrada Familia, financed by public subscription and from 1914 his only occupation. Unfinished, even today, it remains an extraordinary monument to the genius of this intensely individualistic architect. A recent example of individually based imaginative architecture can be found in the work of Austrian artist Friedensreich Hundertwasser (1928–2000) whose residential buildings and churches, such as the Hundertwasser-Haus in Vienna and the St Barbara church at Bärnbach in Styria, are just a few of his revolutionary plans for structures and cities to be transformed into reality.

Jean Dubuffet himself was inspired by the art brut artists to make his own environment at Périgny-sur-Yerres, outside Paris. His Closerie Falballa took two years to construct at a cost of five million francs and employed teams of construction workers. The Closerie Falballa is an overpowering experience as visitors find themselves completely engulfed within a giant Dubuffet painting. The Tarot Garden (see pages 100–107) by Niki de Saint Phalle (1930–2002) is similarly inspired. Much of the construction details were worked out by her partner Jean Tinguely (1925–1991), and completed by workers under their direction. In these cases the highly personal imagery and unique concepts led to stunning results. The kitsch Aw Boon Haw Garden in Hong Kong (see pages 226–227) and The Haw Par Villa in Singapore (see pages 228–231), although the concept of one man, had less of a personal vision and were built as a tourist attraction by local craftsmen. There are folk art precedents for visionary environments in Eastern Europe where folk traditions have survived into the late 20th century. The carved tombstones of Serbia and Bosnia have found a contemporary parallel in Romania where the Sapinta cemetery is a mass of carved and painted wooden memorials, each depicting the deceased with a few lines of poetry. All the work of one man,

Jean Dubuffet wurde von den Werken der »Art-Brut«-Künstler zu einem eigenen Environment in Périgny-sur-Yerres bei Paris inspiriert. Der Bau der Closerie Falballa dauerte zwei Jahre, kostete fünf Millionen Franc und beschäftigte ganze Arbeiterkolonnen. Der Besucher hat den Eindruck, direkt in ein überdimensionales Gemälde von Dubuffet zu treten – eine überwältigende Erfahrung. Der Tarotgarten von Niki de Saint Phalle (1930–2002) ist ähnlich inspirierend (siehe Seite 100–107). Viele Konstruktionselemente wurden von ihrem Lebensgefährten Jean Tinguely (1925–1991) gefertigt, und die Anlage dann unter ihrer Aufsicht von Arbeitern fertiggestellt. Die Closerie Falballa und der Tarotgarten sind herausragende Beispiele für eine sehr persönliche Bildsprache und einzigartige Konzeption. Die kitschigen Aw Boon Haw Gardens in Hongkong (siehe Seite 226–227) und Haw Par Villa in Singapur (siehe Seite 228–231) wurden dagegen zwar ebenfalls von einer einzigen Person erdacht, aber von lokalen Handwerkern als Touristenattraktion errichtet und verraten nicht in demselben Maß eine persönliche visionäre Kraft. In Osteuropa, wo die Volkskunst auch Ende des 20. Jahrhundert noch überlebt hat, finden sich volkstümliche Beispiele der Visionary Environments. In diesem Zusammenhang lassen sich die gemeißelten Grabmäler in Bosnien und Serbien als zeitgenössisches Gegenstück zu dem Friedhof Sapinta in Rumänien nennen. Auf dem rumänischen Friedhof befinden sich zahllose geschnitzte und bemalte Holztafeln, die mit einigen Zeilen der Toten gedenken. Sapinta ist das Werk eines einzigen Mannes: Stan Ion Patras, der ab 1936 den Friedhof in ein Meer aus Farben und Formen verwandelte. Der Kreuzhügel von Litauen hat ebenfalls den Tod zum Thema. Dieses Environment besteht aus Zehntausenden individuell angefertigter Kruzifixe zum Gedenken an ebenso viele Verstorbene.

s'étire sur la terrasse, somptueusement décoré de fragments de céramique multicolores. A la même époque, il réalise la Casa Batlló (1904–1906), demeure aux formes ondoyantes qui évoque plus la sculpture que l'architecture. Son grand œuvre, la cathédrale de la Sagrada Familia, financée par souscription publique, l'occupe entièrement à partir de 1914. Inachevée à ce jour, elle demeure un témoignage extraordinaire du génie de cet esprit indépendant.

L'Autrichien Friedensreich Hundertwasser (1928–2000), crée des architectures aussi personnelles qu'imaginatives, immeubles d'habitation tels que la Hundertwasser-Haus de Vienne, ou églises comme celle de Sainte-Barbara à Bärnbach en Styrie. D'autres projets révolutionnaires de villes et d'édifices attendent de voir le jour.

Jean Dubuffet lui-même n'a pas hésité à créer son propre environnement visionnaire non loin de Paris, à Périgny-sur-Yerres. Sa Closerie Falbala fut réalisée en deux ans, avec un budget de cinq millions de francs; le chantier employa des équipes entières d'ouvriers. Le visiteur a l'impression de pénétrer dans une toile géante de Dubuffet, expérience tout à fait stupéfiante. Le Pardin des Tarots (voir pages 100–107) de Niki de Saint Phalle (1930–2002) se situe dans la même veine: si Jean Tinguely (1925–1991), son partenaire, a mis au point bon nombre d'éléments de construction, le site a été bâti par des ouvriers, sous la direction du tandem. Ces environnements se distinguent par une démarche singulière et une imagerie très personnelle qui ont donné naissance à des réalisations étonnantes. Bien que conçus par un homme seul et construits par des artisans de l'endroit, les très kitsch Aw Boon Haw Gardens de Hong Kong (voir pages 226–227) et Haw Par Villa de Singapour (voir pages 228–231) sont pensés comme des attractions touristiques et relèvent d'une approche moins originale.

En Europe de l'Est où les traditions populaires ont survécu très avant dans le 20e siècle, les environnements visionnaires ont des prédécesseurs. Ainsi les pierres tombales sculptées de Serbie et de Bosnie ont trouvé leur équivalent contemporain en Roumanie, avec le cimetière

Antoni Gaudí,
Parc Güell, Barcelona (1904–1914)

Photo: François René Roland

13

Antoni Gaudí,
Sagrada Familia, Barcelona (1883–1926)

Photo: François René Roland

Stan Ion Patras, who has been working on this unique creation since 1936, the Cemetery at Sapinta is a blaze of colour and decorative forms. The religious theme can also be seen at Lithuania's Hill of Crosses, where tens of thousands of individually made crucifixes contributed by as many people, cram together to form an environment of powerful chaos. One of the great mysteries of visionary environments is the diversity of their geographical location and their particular prevalence in France and the United States. Is it because of the natural individualistic nature of these two nations, both of whom were born out of revolution and regard for individual liberty? Certainly they are less prone to overbearing bureaucratic control and less susceptible to conservative conventions. Both cultures also have a high regard for the art of the people and perhaps this helps these singular creators to find the inner strength they need for their monumental tasks.

The destruction of environments is always a real threat. Clarence Schmidt's vast House of Mirrors, constructed of hundreds of old window frames built around tinsel-covered trees in Woodstock, New York state, was mysteriously burnt down in 1968, with the finger of suspicion pointing at hostile neighbours. Armand Schulthess's Casa Reggio in Ticino, Switzerland, an environment of several acres of signs and messages, was destroyed by embarrassed relatives immediately after his death in 1972. A similar fate befell the Mr H Smith's life-size statues in the Essex village of Matching Green which were quickly disposed once he had died. The city authorities of Newark, New Jersey, successfully destroyed Kea Tawana's Ark in 1988, in spite of a vociferous struggle by her supporters and Tyree Guyton's Heidelberg Project (see pages 164–167) was partly destroyed by the Detroit city authorities. No one will ever know how many undocumented sites have failed to find the protection so often needed to preserve them from ignorant authorities and embarrassed families.

There have also been success stories in the battle for preservation. Efforts by the City of Los Angeles to demolish The Watts Towers in the late 1950s were successfully opposed by a

Eines der größten Rätsel der Visionary Environments ist deren weltweite Verbreitung und das besonders dichte Auftreten in Frankreich und den Vereinigten Staaten. Liegt das an der individualistischen Natur dieser beiden Nationen, die sich ihre Freiheit durch eine Revolution erkämpften? Beide neigen jedenfalls nicht zu einer alles erstickenden bürokratischen Kontrolle oder zu konservativen Konventionen. Beide Nationen haben großen Respekt vor der Volkskunst, und dies hilft wahrscheinlich den Künstlern, die nötige innere Stärke für ihre Werke zu finden.

Den Visionary Environments droht immer wieder die Zerstörung. Clarence Schmidts House of Mirrors, das den Einwohner von Woodstock im Staat New York von jeher ein Dorn im Auge gewesen war, wurde 1968 unter mysteriösen Umständen bei einem Brand vernichtet. Das Haus bestand aus Hunderten alter Fensterrahmen, die um mit Rauschgold bedeckte Bäume herum aufgestellt waren. Die Casa Reggio von Armand Schulthess im Tessin in der Schweiz, ein Environment aus Schildern und Botschaften auf einem Gelände von mehreren Hektar Land, wurde 1972 direkt nach dem Tod des Erbauers von seinen beschämten Angehörigen zerstört. Die lebensgroßen Statuen von H. Smith in dem Dorf Matching Green in Essex fielen einem ähnlichen Schicksal zum Opfer und wurden kurz nach seinem Tod schnell entfernt. Die Behörden von Newark in New Jersey demontierten 1988 die Arche von Kea Tawana trotz lautstarker Proteste der Anhänger, und kürzlich erst riß die Stadtverwaltung von Detroit das Heidelberg Project (siehe Seite 164–167) von Tyree Guyton teilweise ab. Niemand weiß, wie viele undokumentierte Visionary Environments schon von ignoranten Behörden und aufgebrachten Angehörigen zerstört worden sind.

Aber viele Visionary Environments konnten auch erhalten werden. Als die Stadt Los Angeles in den späten fünfziger Jahren die Watts Towers abreißen lassen wollte, konnte sich ein eigens gebildetes Komitee gegen die Behörden durchsetzen. Und heute veranlaßten dieselben Behörden eine umfangreiche Restaurierung.

de Sapinta, dédale de monuments funéraires en bois sculpté et peint où quelques vers de poésie évoquent chaque mort. Œuvre d'un seul homme, Stan Ion Patras, qui entreprit cette tâche en 1936, Sapinta est un feu d'artifice de couleurs et de formes. De même, la Colline des Croix, en Lituanie, croule sous des dizaines de milliers de crucifix fabriqués artisanalement par autant de personnes, qui se pressent en un chaos d'une force rare.

L'un des grands mystères des environnements visionnaires est leur présence un peu partout dans le monde et leur nombre particulièrement élevé en France et aux Etats-Unis. Faut-il y voir le reflet de la nature individualiste de ces deux nations, nées d'une révolution et du respect des libertés individuelles? Les deux pays semblent en tout cas moins portés vers un contrôle asphyxiant du paysage et moins soumis aux convenances. De plus, ils font preuve de la même considération pour l'art populaire, ce qui donne peut-être aux créateurs singuliers la force intérieure dont ils ont besoin pour mener à bien leurs entreprises monumentales.

Quantité d'environnements visionnaires sont menacés de destruction. A Woodstock, dans l'Etat de New York, la grande House of Mirrors de Clarence Schmidt, où des centaines de vieilles fenêtres formaient une maison autour d'arbres recouverts de papier aluminium, a mystérieusement brûlé en 1968: faut-il soupçonner le voisinage hostile? Décor de plusieurs hectares parsemé de pancartes et d'inscriptions, la Casa Reggio d'Armand Schulthess, dans le Tessin suisse, a été détruite à la mort de son créateur, par des héritiers gênés d'avoir dans leur famille pareil original. Un sort similaire a frappé les statues grandeur nature créées par H. Smith à Matching Green, un village de l'Essex. La municipalité de Newark, dans le New Jersey, est parvenue à détruire l'arche de

specially formed committee of supporters and today those same authorities are carrying out an expensive programme of restoration. Preservation organisations such as the Los Angeles-based SPACES and the Kansas Grassroots Art Association have been instrumental in both physically saving places from destruction and decay and raising the awareness of both public and government. One environment, built completely inside a large house by Annie Hooper in North Carolina, consisted of thousands of Biblical figures acting out epic scenes from the scriptures. Every room of the house was so full that there remained just a narrow path through the Biblical hoards. On her death, the Jargon Society were able to finance the rescue of all the figures and in the future a permanent exhibition space will be made for them. Another organisation, the Kohler Foundation Inc. in Wisconsin, have funded ambitious restoration projects, including The Wisconsin Concrete Park by Fred Smith (1886–1976) and The Prairie Moon Sculpture Garden and Museum (see pages 184–185) by Herman Rusch (1885–1985) and have also created a special Nek Chand sculpture garden at its Art Center. The Orange Show, an environment in Houston created by Jeff McKissack (1902-1979), is now a thriving centre for self-taught art which organises the famous annual Art Car Parade.

The American Visionary Art Museum, which opened in 1991 in Baltimore, is proposing to create a permanent home for threatened environments. The planned final phase of this huge museum, to be named Visionary Village, will become a haven for backyard and major environments which find themselves in need of protection and long term preservation. This ambition has

Hundertwasser – Peter Pelikan,
Colour Scheme for the Hundertwasser House, Kegelgasse Side, Vienna
Fassadenplan für das Hundertwasser-Haus, Ansicht Kegelgasse, Wien
Plan de la façade de la maison Hundertwasser, vue de la Kegelgasse, Vienne (1985)

Organisationen wie die SPACES in Los Angeles und die Kansas Grassroots Art Association haben viele Environments vor Verfall sowie Zerstörung bewahrt und gleichzeitig das Interesse der Öffentlichkeit und der Behörden wecken können.

In dem großen Haus von Annie Hooper in North Carolina standen Tausende von biblischen Figuren, die nur einen schmalen Pfad im Haus freiließen. Nach ihrem Tod konnte die Jargon Society alle Skulpturen retten und wird sie demnächst in einer Dauerausstellung öffentlich zugänglich machen. Auch die Kohler Foundation Inc. in Wisconsin hat aufwendige Restaurierungen finanziert, darunter Wisconsin Concrete Park von Fred Smith (1886–1976) und Prairie Moon Sculpture Garden and Museum (siehe Seite 184–185) von Herman Rusch (1885–1985). Darüber hinaus verfügt das Art Center seit einiger Zeit über eine Sammlung von 160 Figuren, die aus dem Skulpturengarten von Nek Chand stammen. Die Orange Show von Jeff McKissack (1902–1979) in Houston entwickelte sich zu einem sehr aktiven Zentrum für autodidaktische Kunst und organisiert jedes Jahr die bekannte Art Car Parade.

Das American Visionary Art Museum, das 1991 in Baltimore vorläufig eröffnet wurde und nach seiner endgültigen Fertigstellung Visionary Village heißen wird, soll kleine und größere von Zerstörung und Verfall bedrohte Environments aufnehmen. Ein ähnliches Museum gibt es schon in Caen, wo 1997 der Jardin de la Luna Rossa eröffnet wurde. Hier werden gerettete Statuen und Stücke aus Visionary Environments und Skulpturengärten gesammelt, repariert und ausgestellt.

Vielleicht die aufsehenerregendste Auseinandersetzung wurde um das größte Environment ausgetragen, den Skulpturengarten von Nek Chand in den Außenbezirken der nordindischen Stadt Chandigarh, die der Schweizer Architekt Le Corbusier in den fünfziger und sechziger Jahren errichtet hatte. Chand arbeitete nachts heimlich beim Licht von brennenden Autorreifen und schuf auf einer Lichtung sein Reich von

Kea Tawana en 1988, malgré les protestations vigoureuses de ses défenseurs. Récemment, la municipalité de Détroit en a fait autant, du moins partiellement, pour le Heidelberg Project de Tyree Guyton (voir pages 164–167). Personne ne saura jamais combien de sites anonymes n'ont jamais trouvé protection contre des autorités ignorantes ou des familles embarrassées.

Mais il y a aussi des victoires. Les tentatives de la municipalité de Los Angeles pour démolir les tours de Watts, dans les années 1950, ont été contrées avec succès par un comité de défense et, aujourd'hui, les autorités de la ville font restaurer à grands frais cette structure. Des organisations de sauvegarde telles que SPACES, à Los Angeles, ou la Kansas Grassroots Art Association, ont joué un rôle considérable sur deux fronts, préservation des sites menacés de ruine ou de destruction, et sensibilisation du public comme des autorités.

La Jargon Society a volé au secours du peuple biblique d'Annie Hooper, en Caroline du Nord. L'installation occupait une vaste maison et comptait des milliers

Stan Ion Patras,
Cemetery of Sapinta, Romania
Friedhof von Sapinta, Rumänien
Le Cimetière de Sapinta, Roumanie

Photo: Beryl Sokoloff

de personnages réunis dans des scènes tirées des Ecritures; cette foule emplissait chaque pièce, laissant tout juste un passage étroit pour circuler. A la mort de Hooper, la Jargon Society a pu financer le sauvetage de tous les personnages, qu'un espace d'exposition permanente devrait abriter dans l'avenir. Dans le Wisconsin, la Kohler Foundation Inc. a financé d'importants projets de restauration, dont ceux du Wisconsin Concrete Park de Fred Smith (1886–1976), et du Prairie Moon Sculpture Garden and Museum (voir pages 184–185) de Herman Rusch (1885–1985). La fondation a aussi créé, dans son centre des arts, un jardin où se dressent 160 des sculptures de Nek Chand. Le Orange Show, environnement créé à Houston par Jeff McKissack (1902–1979), abrite désormais un centre très actif consacré à l'art autodidacte, qui organise chaque année la célèbre Art Car Parade.

15

already been realised in France, where an open air art brut museum, Le Jardin de Luna Rossa, opened in Caen in 1997. It collects rescued sculptures and elements from environments and sculpture gardens, bringing them to their charming new home to be repaired and cared for. Perhaps the most epic struggle for survival centres on the largest of all the environments. Nek Chand's forest clearing on the outskirts of Chandigarh, a new city which constructed in the Fifties and Sixties by the great Swiss architect Le Corbusier, was technically illegal. He worked in secret at night by the light of burning tyres, laying out his kingdom of kings and queens, courtiers and village people. When his creation was eventually discovered in 1972, it consisted of countless hundreds of life-size figures and beasts as well as thousands of stones. Nek Chand had been working in an area where all development was forbidden. By rights his creation should have been destroyed, and although some in the Chandigarh Administration echoed this demand, he also had much support. After two years of

indecision, during which time his environment grew dramatically as people flocked to donate materials, the authorities decided that The Rock Garden could remain. Shortly afterwards Nek Chand was relieved of his duties as a roads inspector, given a salary, a truck and a small workforce to help him in his ambitious construction programme. With this new assistance he was able to build huge waterfall sculptures, made-made gorges, vast arches and walls, and to cover acres of ground with mosaics of broken ceramics.

However, in more recent years the City cut off his funding. Bulldozers arrived at the gates of the The Rock Garden in 1989 to clear the way for a VIP road for the use of top bureaucrats. Protesters included children who lay down to block the machinery and a lengthy court action eventually judged in Nek Chand's favour. In 1996 enemies in the local administration withdrew his dwindling workforce the day

Königen und Königinnen, Höflingen und Dorfbewohnern. Bei seiner Entdeckung 1972 bestand das Werk aus zahllosen lebensgroßen Figuren und Tierskulpturen sowie Tausenden von Steinen.

Nek Chands Welt befand sich in einem Gebiet, in dem Bauen und Bewirtschaften strikt verboten war. Von Rechts wegen hätte sein Werk abgetragen werden müssen. Obwohl einige Mitglieder der örtlichen Behörden diese Vorgehensweise befürworteten, sprachen sich andere für den Erhalt seiner Arbeit aus. Die Diskussionen dauerten zwei Jahre an. In diesem Zeitraum wuchs der Skulpturengarten immer mehr an, weil Chand mit gespendeten Baumaterialien regelrecht überhäuft wurde. Die Behörden stimmten schließlich der Erhaltung des Rock Garden of Chandigarh zu. Kurze Zeit später wurde Chand von seinen Pflichten als Straßenbauinspektor befreit. Die Stadt zahlte ihm ein Gehalt, finanzierte einen LKW und diverse Hilfskräfte für die weitere Arbeit an dem ehrgeizigen Projekt. Mit diesen Mitteln gestaltete Chand beeindruckende Skulpturen und Wasserfälle, legte künstliche Schluchten an, errichtete gewaltige Bögen und Mauern und bedeckte etliche Hektar Bodenfläche mit Mosaiken aus farbenprächtigen Keramikscherben.

Doch einige Jahre später machte die Stadt ihre finanzielle Unterstützung rückgängig. Bulldozer ebneten 1989 einen Teil der Anlage ein zugunsten einer Zufahrtsstraße für hohe Beamte. Dies wurde mit zahlreichen Protestaktionen quittiert; so legten sich Kinder vor die Baufahrzeuge. Eine langwierige Gerichtsverhandlung endete schließlich zu Chands Gunsten. Doch 1996 zogen Chands Gegner in der Stadtverwaltung einen Tag nach dessen Abreise zu einem längeren Auslandsaufenthalt die Hilfskräfte ab. Bei seiner Rückkehr mußte der Künstler feststellen, daß Hunderte von Statuen zerstört worden waren. Die Folge war ein internationaler Skandal, der schließlich zur Gründung der Nek Chand Foundation führte. Die Organisation traf eine Vereinbarung mit der Stadt Chandigarh, die das künftige Fortbestehen des Rock Garden of Chandigarh garantiert.

Inauguré en 1991 à Baltimore, le American Visionary Art Museum se propose d'accueillir à titre permanent des environnements menacés. Lorsque ce lieu énorme, un ancien entrepôt rebaptisé Visionary Village, sera achevé, il deviendra un havre pour des ensembles petits et grands nécessitant protection et entretien. Un projet du même ordre a déjà vu le jour en France avec le Jardin de la Luna Rossa, à Caen, musée d'art brut à ciel ouvert créé en 1997. Il collecte des œuvres et des éléments provenant d'environnements visionnaires et de jardins de sculptures, les répare et leur offre son cadre charmant. Le combat le plus épique pour la préservation d'un site a sans doute été celui mené en faveur du plus vaste environnement visionnaire au monde, le Jardin de pierres de Nek Chand. Situé dans une clairière aux abords de Chandigarh, ville nouvelle construite par l'architecte suisse Le Corbusier dans les années cinquante et

Clarence Schmidt,
House of Mirrors, Woodstock N. Y.

Photo: Delphine Piovant

soixante, le site était illégal. Nek Chand travaillait en secret la nuit, à la lumière de pneus qu'il faisait brûler, aménageant son univers de rois et de reines, de courtisans et de villageois. Quand les autorités découvrirent l'œuvre en 1972, celle-ci se composait déjà de centaines de statues grandeur nature d'hommes et d'animaux, ainsi que de milliers de pierres.

L'administration de Chandigarh pouvait faire raser cet environnement bâti sur un terrain inconstructible mais Nek Chand avait quantité de défenseurs. Après deux ans d'hésitations, au cours desquels le site s'agrandit considérablement grâce à de nombreux dons de matériaux de construction, les autorités municipales donnèrent droit de cité au jardin. Mieux encore, elles déchargèrent Nek Chand de sa tâche officielle et lui accordèrent un salaire pour qu'il puisse poursuivre son œuvre; enfin, elles lui fournirent un camion et une petite équipe. Ces moyens lui permirent de construire de grandes arcades, des murs, de gigantesques cascades, et de

after he left for a visit abroad, leaving The Rock Garden unguarded. When he returned he found that hundreds of statues had been vandalised. The international outrage that ensued resulted in the establishment of the Nek Chand Foundation, which secured an agreement from the Chandigarh Administration to protect The Rock Garden's future existence.

The true outsider artist works from no drawing or plan. Their constructions grow organically, a living and ever developing creation. For their materials they use whatever they have at hand. Cement is usually the only material that needs to be purchased. They use broken crockery, stones and flints, scrap iron, wire, driftwood, mud, old dolls, old cars, hubcaps, demolition reclaims, window frames, glass bottles, roots. They are endlessly inventive, each finding materials that are free and plentiful, be it dug up from river beds or rescued from a nearby rubbish tip. Nek Chand has even used human hair, broken bangles, fluorescent light tubes, iron foundry slag, plastic plug moulds, and cooking pots. It is not unusual to find huge piles of reclaimed materials around the back of these creations while in progress: the "storeroom" beside the "studio" of these strongly independent visionary creators.

A visit to a major visionary environment is an overwhelming experience. While at an art gallery one can look through the "window" of a painting into the artist's imagination, the visitor walking through an environment is actually within the fantasy world the artist has created. Surrounded on all sides by powerful creative vision, the viewer has stepped into an alternative reality, a reality that is no figment of the imagination but one that actually exists. These untutored geniuses have created a unique artform. Their years of commitment to a single massive work put to shame many who call themselves "artist", a term that few of these extraordinary creators would use for themselves. Humble and yet proud, they are seldom in doubt of their power, their uniqueness and their value to the world.

Ein wahrer Outsider-Künstler führt seine Arbeit ohne Skizzen und Pläne aus. Sein Werk versteht sich als lebendige und organisch wachsende Schöpfung. Als Baumaterial wird alles verwendet, was zur Verfügung steht. Oft ist Zement das einzige Material, das die Künstler tatsächlich kaufen. Ansonsten verwenden sie zerbrochenes Geschirr, Steine, Feuersteine, Altmetall, Draht, Treibholz, Lehm, alte Puppen, ausrangierte Autos, Radkappen, Schrottplatzfunde, Fensterrahmen, Glasflaschen, Wurzeln und ähnliches. Jeder dieser Künstler ist unendlich einfallsreich und macht Materialien ausfindig, die in der näheren Umgebung kostenlos und reichlich vorhanden sind – gleichgültig ob sie aus einem Flußbett ausgehoben oder von der örtlichen Mülldeponie bezogen werden. Nek Chand verwendete sogar Menschenhaar, zerbrochene Armreifen, Neonröhren, Schlacke einer Eisengießerei, Gießformen für Plastiksteckdosen und Kochtöpfe. Solange die Arbeit andauert, sind Unmengen aufgestapelter Altmaterialien in der Nähe der Visionary Environments keine Seltenheit: Sie dienen als Materiallager neben dem »Atelier« der größtenteils völlig eigenständig arbeitenden Künstler.

Der Besuch eines Visionary Environment ist eine überwältigende Erfahrung. In einer Galerie blickt man beim Betrachten eines Gemäldes wie durch ein Fenster in die Innenwelt des Künstlers. Bei der Besichtigung eines Environment dagegen betritt der Besucher eine von dem Künstler geschaffene Phantasiewelt. Umgeben von kraftvollen Visionen befindet er sich in einer anderen Realität. Gemeinsam haben diese Genies, die nie eine künstlerische Ausbildung genossen haben, eine einzigartige Kunstform geschaffen. Die in vielen Jahre völliger Hingabe geschaffenen Werke stellen die Arbeiten mancher der anerkannten Künstler in den Schatten. Allerdings würden nur wenige dieser außergewöhnlichen Menschen sich selbst »Künstler« nennen. Trotz dieser Bescheidenheit sind sie sich voller Stolz ihrer Stärke, ihrer Einzigartigkeit und ihrer Bedeutung für die Welt sehr wohl bewußt.

creuser des ravins et des gorges; il couvrit également des hectares de terrain avec des mosaïques en céramique cassée.

Nouveau rebondissement en 1989. La municipalité interrompt ses subventions tandis que des bulldozers se présentent à l'entrée du site: ils doivent dégager la voie pour construire une route à l'usage des hauts fonctionnaires. Des manifestants, parmi lesquels des enfants, se couchent devant les engins. A l'issue d'une longue procédure, Nek Chand obtient un jugement en sa faveur. En 1996 enfin, alors qu'il se trouve à l'étranger, les autorités rappellent son équipe réduite, laissant le site sans surveillance. A son retour, il découvre que des centaines de statues ont subi des dégradations. Le scandale provoqué en Inde et ailleurs a pour résultat la création de la fondation Nek Chand; celle-ci a obtenu que la municipalité protège désormais le Jardin de pierres.

Le véritable artiste brut travaille sans plan ni croquis. Ensemble vivant, son œuvre croît organiquement. Ces créateurs se servent de ce qu'ils ont sous la main. Bien souvent, ils n'achètent que le ciment et récupèrent le reste: vaisselle cassée, pierres, silex, métal, fil de fer, bois flottés, vieilles poupées, carcasses de voitures, enjoliveurs, rebuts de chantiers de démolition, cadres de fenêtres, bouteilles en verre, racines. Ils font preuve d'une imagination sans bornes, trouvant chacun selon le lieu un matériau gratuit et abondant, tiré d'un lit de rivière ou d'une décharge locale. Nek Chand a même utilisé des cheveux humains, des bracelets cassés, des tubes fluorescents, des scories de fonderie, des moules de prises électriques en plastique, des casseroles. Bien souvent, d'énormes piles de matériaux de récupération s'entassent à l'arrière d'un site en cours de réalisation, réserve alimentant l'«atelier» de ces artistes si indépendants dans leur démarche.

La découverte d'un environnement visionnaire constitue une expérience saisissante. Dans un musée ou une galerie, on entre par la «fenêtre» du tableau dans l'imagination de l'artiste. Ici, on s'aventure de plain-pied dans un univers fantastique, dans une réalité parallèle, inventée de toutes pièces mais concrète. Elle est l'œuvre de génies sans bagage culturel qui ont su inventer une forme de création unique, consacrant à la même réalisation un temps infini, ce dont bien des artistes, au sens officiel, ne peuvent se vanter. Modestes mais fiers, ils doutent rarement de leur force, de leur singularité et de leur valeur dans le monde.

The appendix mentions only those visionary environments that are open to the public. The addresses of environments that have been destroyed or are not open to the public are not included. Many of the addresses given here are of private residences. In some cases, the artists have moved and property in the visionary environment has changed hands. Sites should therefore be approached with circumspection and proper respect for the current occupants.

Im Anhang sind nur die öffentlich zugänglichen Visionary Environments verzeichnet. Er enthält nicht die Adressen von Environments, die inzwischen zerstört worden oder nicht öffentlich zugänglich sind. Viele der hier aufgeführten Adressen sind Privatadressen. In einigen Fällen wohnen die Künstler selbst nicht mehr dort, vielmehr sind die Environments in den Besitz anderer Privatpersonen übergegangen. Rücksichtnahme auf die Bewohner ist daher bei Besichtigungen unbedingt angebracht.

L'annexe mentionne uniquement les environnements visionnaires publiques. Les adresses des environnements qui ont été détruits entretemps ou qui ne sont pas ouverts au public ne sont pas citées. Un grand nombre des adresses sont des habitations privées. Dans quelques cas, les artistes eux-mêmes n'habitent plus sur place et les propriétés où se trouvent les environnements appartiennent à d'autres personnes. Nous recommandons de visiter ces lieux avec le respect et les précautions qui s'imposent.

EUROPE / EUROPA

La Bohème, Lucien Favreau
Visit on appointment
Madame Mireille Dussuel
Yviers
F–16210 Chalais
Tel. +33–(0)5 45 98 02 65

Il Castello incantato, Filippo Bentivegna
Via Ghezzi
I–92019 Sciacca (Agrigento)
Tel. +39–0925–99 30 44
Tel. +39–0925–20 478

La Cathédrale, Jean Linard
Les Poteries
F–18250 Neuvy-Deux-Clochers
(40 km NE of Bourges)
Tel. +33–(0)2 48 26 73 87

Cunégonde et Malabar, Ben Vautier
Ben et sa maison
103, route de Saint-Pancrace
F–06100 Nice
www.ben-vautier.com

Le Cyclop, Jean Tinguely and Niki de Saint Phalle
Visit on appointment
Please contact the tourist office of
Milly-La-Forêt for further information
F–91490 Milly-La-Forêt
Tel. +33–(0)1 64 98 83 17

La Demeure aux figures, Roland Dutel
Place des Tilleuls
F–26220 Dieulefit
Tel. +33–(0)4 75 46 86 84

Gillis à Barras, Jean Prosper Gillis
Bonaguil
F–47500 Saint-Front-sur-Lémance
(5 km from Fumel)
Tel. +33–(0)5 53 40 65 54

Das Haus der Künstler, August Walla, Oswald Tschirtner, Johann Garber etc.
Landesnervenklinik
Hauptstr. 2
A–3400 Maria Gugging
Tel. +43–(0)2243–87992
www.gugging.org

L'Hélice terrestre, Jacques Warminski
Association d'Art plastique permanente
Village troglodytique de l'Orbière
F–49350 Saint-Georges-des-Sept-Voies
(35 km SE of Angers)
Tel. +33–(0)2 41 57 95 92
Fax +33–(0)2 41 57 95 12

Le Jardin coquillage, Bodan Litnianski
15, rue Jean-Jaurès
Viry-Noureuil
F–02300 Chauny

Le Jardin sculpté d'Albert Gabriel, Albert Gabriel
Chez Audebert
F–17770 Nantillé (on D 129)

Le Jardin zoologique, Emile Taugourdeau
F–72800 Thorée-les-Pins (6 km from La Flèche)

Das Junkerhaus, Karl Junker
Hamelner Str. 36
D–32657 Lemgo
Tel. +49–(0)5261–66 76 95
www.junkerhaus.de

The Little Chapel, Frère Déodat
Les Vauxbelets
St. Andrews
GB–Guernsey
www.thelittlechapel.org
Tel. +44–(0)1481–23 72 00

La Maison à vaisselle cassée, Robert Vasseur
80, rue du Bal-champêtre
F–27400 Louviers
Tel. +33–(0)2 32 40 22 71

La Maison de Celle-qui-peint, Danielle Jacqui
Pont-de-l'Etoile
F–13360 Roquevaire
Tel. +33–(0)4 42 04 25 32

La Maison Picassiette, Raymond Isidore
22, rue du Repos
Saint-Chéron
F–27000 Chartres
Tel. +33–(0)2 37 34 10 78
Tel. +33–(0)2 37 90 45 80
Fax +33–(0)2 37 90 45 90
musee.beaux-arts@ville-chartres.fr

Le Manège, Pierre Avezard
La Fabuloserie
F–89120 Dicy
(27 km E of Montargis)
Tel. +33–(0)3 86 63 64 21
www.fabuloserie.com

Le Musée Communal Robert Tatin
Maison des Champs
La Frénouse
F–53230 Cossé-le-Vivien
Tel. +33–(0)2 43 98 80 89

Le Palais idéal, Ferdinand Cheval
F–26390 Hauterives
Tel. +33–(0)4 75 68 81 19
www.facteurcheval.com

Le Parc-exposition Raymond Morales
Musée Morales
Route de Fos
Avenue des Pins - Z.I La grand colle
F–13110 Port-de-Bouc
Tel. +33–(0)4 42 06 49 01

Il Parco dei Tarocchi, Niki de Saint Phalle
Località Garavicchio
I–58011 Capalbio
Tel. +39–0564–89 51 22
www.nikidesaintphalle.com

Les Rochers sculptés, Abbé Adolphe Julien Fouré
Chemin des Rochers sculptés
Rothéneuf
F–35400 Saint-Malo
Tel. +33–(0)2 99 56 23 95
Tel. +33–(0)6 68 98 23 95

La Scarzuola, Tomaso Buzzi
I–05010 Montegabbione (TR)
Tel. +39–0763–83 74 63

The Sedlec Ossuary, František Rint
Kostnice-Sedlec
Zámecká 127
CZ–28403 Kutná Hora
Tel. +42–(0)728–12 54 88
www.kostnice.cz

La Tour de l'Apocalypse, Robert Garcet
Musée du Silex asbl
B–4690 Eben-Emael
(8 km S of Maastricht)
Tel. +32–(0)4–286 92 70
www.musee-du-silex.be

The Josef Váchal Museum, Josef Váchal
CZ–57001 Litomyšl-Záhrad
Terézy Novákové 75
Tel. +42–(0)461–61 20 20

Le Village d'Art préludien, Chomo
Visit on appointment
24, rue d'Archères-la-Forêt
F–77116 Ury
(on D 63)

Der Weinrebenpark, Bruno Weber and Marianne Weber-Prot
Zur Weinrebe
CH–8953 Dietikon
Fax +41–(0)44–740 02 71
www.bruno-weber.com

AMÉRICA / AMÉRIKA / AMÉRIQUE

The Art Yard, Richard Tracy
203 M Street
USA–Centralia, Washington 98531
Tel. +1–360–736 79 90

The Coral Castle, Edward Leedskalnin
28655 South Dixie Highway
USA–Homestead, Florida 33030
Tel. +1–305–248 63 44
www.coralcastle.com

The Desert Sculpture Garden, Noah Purifoy
Visit on appointment
63030 Blair Lane
USA–Joshua Tree, California 92252
Tel. +1-213-382 75 16
www.noahpurifoy.com

The Desert View Tower, Bert L. Vaughn and MT Radcliffe
off I-8 on In-Ko-Pah
USA–Jacumba, California 91934
Tel. +1–619–766 46 12

The Dickeyville Grotto, Father Mathias Wernerus
305 West Main Street
USA–Dickeyville, Wisconsin 53808
Tel. +1–608–568 31 19

Forevertron, Tom O. Every
P.O. Box 103
USA–Prairie du Sac, Wisconsin 53578
Half way between Prairie du Sac and Baraboo, Wisconsin on Highway 12
Tel. +1–608–643 80 09

The Garden of Eden, Samuel Perry Dinsmoor
Kansas and Second Street
USA–Lucas, Kansas 67648
Tel. +1–785–(0)3 86 93 95
www.garden-of-eden-lucas-kansas.com

The Grotto of the Redemption, Father Paul Dobberstein
300 North Broadway
P.O. Box 376
USA–West Bend, Iowa 50597
Tel. +1–515–887 23 71
www.westbendgrotto.com

The Heidelberg Project, Tyree Guyton
3360 Charlevoix (office)
USA–Detroit, Michigan 48207
Tel. +1–313–267 16 22
www.heidelberg.org

The Junk Castle, Bobby and Vic Moore
502 Armstrong Road
USA–Pullman, Washington 99163
(3 miles W of Pullman off Highway 195)

Mary Nohl's, Mary Nohl
USA–Wisconsin
For information please contact the Kohler Foundation Inc.
Tel. +1–920–458 19 72

Oiseaux Chausse Gros, Richard Greaves
494 Rang Chausse-Gros
St-Simon-les-Mines
CND–Beauce Québec GOM IKO

The Paradise Garden, Howard Finster
P.O. Box 413
Pennville Community
USA–Summerville, Georgia 30747
Tel. +1–205–587 30 90
www.finstersparadisegardens.org

Pasaquan, Eddie Owens Martin
Eddie Martin Road
P.O. Box 564
USA–Buena Vista, Georgia 31803
Tel. +1–229–649 94 44
www.pasaquan.com

Las Pozas, Edward James
Posada El Castillo
MEX–Xilitla, S.L.P.
Tel. +52–489–365 00 38
Fax +52–489–365 00 55
www.junglegossip.com

The Prairie Moon Sculpture Garden and Museum, Herman Rusch
52727 Prairie Moon Road
USA–Cochrane, Wisconsin 54629
Tel. +1–608–687 98 74

The Salvation Mountain, Leonard Knight
Main Street
The Road to Slab City
P.O. Box 298
USA–Niland, California 92257
www.salvationmountain.us

The Thunder Mountain Monument, Rolling Mountain Thunder
On I-80 Exit 145
USA–Imlay, Nevada
Tel. +1–702–538 74 02
www.thundermountainmonument.com

The Totem Pole Park, Nathan Edward Galloway
NE of Tulsa on State Route 28A
USA–Foyil, Oklahoma
Tel. +1–918–342 91 49

The Watts Towers, Simon Rodia
Watts Towers Art Center
1727 East 107th Street
USA–Los Angeles, California 90002
Tel. +1–213–847 46 46
www.wattstowers.org or www.wattstowers.us

The Windmill Park, Vollis Simpson
Box 362, Route 1
Junction of Crossroads 1103 and 1109
USA–Lucama, North Carolina 27851

ASIA / ASIEN / ASIE

The Rock Garden of Chandigarh, Nek Chand Saini
Sector No. 1
Chandigarh (U.T.)
India
Tel. +91–172–740 645
www.nekchand.com

The Buddha Park Garden, Luangpu Boonlour Sureerat
Vientiane, Laos
24 km from Vientiane down stream

The Wat Khaek Buddha Park, Luangpu Boonlour Sureerat
10 Bansamukkee Mang District
Nong Khai
Thailand

The Wat Thawet Learning Garden, Phra Sumroeng
113 Wat Thawet
M.4, T. Tuphoung
Srisumrong District
Sukhothai 64120
Thailand
Tel. +66–55–613 240

The Aw Boon Haw Gardens, Aw Boon Haw
Hong Kong
Closed

Addressen Adressen Adresses

The Haw Par Villa, *Aw Boon Haw*
262 Pasir Panjang Road
Singapore 118628
Tel. +65–774 03 00
Tel. +65–779 12 03

AFRICA / AFRIKA / AFRIQUE

Aeroplane, *Punch Mbhele*
Bergville 3350
South Africa
38 km from Bergville towards Royal Natal
National Park, 2 km from Tower of Pizza

The Owl House, *Helen Martins*
River Street
Nieu-Bethesda 6286
South Africa
Tel. +27–49–841 16 03
Tel. +27–49–841 17 33
www.owlhouse.co.za

ORGANISATIONS AND INSTITUTIONS

GREAT BRITAIN

Raw Vision

1 Watford Road
Radlett
GB-Herts WD7 8LA
Tel. +44–(0)1923–85 66 44
www.rawvision.com
Headquarters of the international Outsider Art
magazine, offering a selection of books and
articles. It is also the base for the British Nek
Chand collection of environmental sculptures.

The Nek Chand Foundation

1 Watford Road
Radlett
GB-Herts WD7 8LA
Tel. +44–(0)1923–85 66 44
www.nekchand.com
Formed to protect and preserve the Rock Garden
of Chandigarh. Fundraising, financing,
information and volunteer programme.

FRANCE

Halle Saint Pierre

2, rue Ronsard
F–75018 Paris
Tel. +33–(0)1 42 58 72 89
www.hallesaintpierre.org
Exhibition centre for Outsider Art and extensive
specialist bookshop.

La Fabuloserie

F–89120 Dicy
Tel. +33–(0)3 86 63 64 21
www.fabuloserie.com
Large private collection of Outsider Art including
park with environmental pieces and the
reconstructed Manège of Pierre Avezard.

Le Jardin de la Luna Rossa

6, rue Damozanne
F–14000 Caen
Open air museum of rescued sculptures and
environmental pieces. Open Sundays from April
to September.

SWITZERLAND

Collection de l'Art Brut

Chateau de Beaulieu
11, avenue des Bergières
CH–1004 Lausanne
Tel. +41–(0)21–315 25 70
www.artbrut.ch
Jean Dubuffet's original collection is housed in a
dramatic purpose-built museum, and supplies
videos and information on environments.

USA

American Visionary Art Museum

800 Key Highway
Inner Harbor
USA–Baltimore, Maryland 21230
Tel. +1–410–244 19 00
Fax +1–410–244 58 58
www.avam.org
America's first museum specialising in Outsider
and Visionary Art, concentrates on large themed
exhibitions, also has permanent sculptural
installations, library and planned environment
wing.

Folk Art Society of America

P.O. Box 17041
USA–Richmond, Virginia 23226
Tel. +1–800–527 36 55
www.folkart.org
An organisation dedicated to furthering
knowledge and awareness of folk art and its
artists, it organises events and conferences.

INTUIT

756 North Milwaukee Avenue
USA–Chicago, Illinois 60622
Tel. +1–312–243 90 88
www.art.org
Organises exhibitions, publishes newsletter, and
hopes to establish an Outsider Art museum.

The Jargon Society

P.O. Box 15458
USA–Winston-Salem, North Carolina 27113
www.jargonbooks.com
Conservation and publications.

Kansas Grassroots Art Center

213 South Main Street
P.O. Box 304
USA–Lucas, Kansas 67648
Tel. +1–785–525 61 18
www.grassrootsart.net
Organisation dedicated to the preservation of
environments and other grassroots expressions.
Has its own museum in Vinland which is moving
to Lucas, Kansas.

Kohler Foundation

725 X Woodlake Road
USA–Kohler, Wisconsin 53044
Tel. +1–920–458 19 72
Funds the restoration of major sites,
documentation and gifting of sites to local
communities. Exhibitions of environmental
sculptures and permanent installation of Nek
Chand.

John Michael Kohler Arts Center

725 X Woodlake Road
USA–Kohler, Wisconsin 53044
Tel. +1–920–458 61 44
www.jmkac.org

The Orange Show Center for Visionary Art

2402 Mungar Street
USA–Houston, Texas 77023
Tel. +1–713–926 63 68
www.orangeshow.org
Dedicated to the care of the Orange Show
environment, also holds regular cultural events
including the Art Car parades, and publishes a
newsletter.

Preserve Bottle Village Committee

Box 1412
USA–Simi Valley, California 93062
Tel. +1–805–584 05 72
http://users.adelphia.net/~echomatic/bv/
contact.html
Formed to aid the preservation of Grandma
Prisbrey's Bottle Village.

SPACES, *Saving and Preserving Arts and*
Cultural Environments

1804 North Van Ness
USA–Los Angeles, California 90028
Tel. +1–323–463 16 29
Principal US preservation organisation.

Europe

La Bo hème

Yviers, France

Der ehemalige Gipser **Lucien Favreau** (1912–1990) widmete seinen Skulpturengarten in Aquitanien Persönlichkeiten und Ereignissen, die er als Zeitzeuge kannte und erlebte. In dem Garten, der zwischen 1963 und 1986 entstand, finden sich die Sänger Mireille Mathieu und Georges Brassens, der Staatsmann Charles de Gaulle, ein Fresko für die Opfer von Treblinka und eine mit einem Herzen verzierte Zementhand als Hommage an den französischen Komiker Coluche. Favreaus Hund Zappy ist hier beerdigt, und inzwischen ruht auch der Künstler selbst zwischen seinen Werken. Das Haus ist innen vollständig mit Fresken und Reliefs verziert: So tummelt sich im Schlafzimmer eine nackte junge Frau neben Schmetterlingen, anderen Tieren und Meereswesen.

The sculpture garden of the former plasterer **Lucien Favreau** (1912–1990) in Aquitaine is dedicated to the public figures and events that marked his long life. Singers Mireille Mathieu and Georges Brassens rub shoulders with statesmen such as Charles de Gaulle, while a fresco commemorates the victims of Treblinka. A hand stands embellished with a heart in homage to the French comedian Coluche. Favreau's beloved dog Zappy has its own tomb, and the artist built one for himself too, so that he could rest in peace amid his own creations, executed between 1963 and 1986. The house is full of frescoes and reliefs; Favreau's bedroom is embellished with the statue of a beautiful young nude and with ornamental butterflies, beasts and aquatic life.

Ancien plâtrier, **Lucien Favreau** (1912–1990) évoque dans son jardin de sculptures en Aquitaine les personnalités et les événements qui l'ont marqué. Les chanteurs Mireille Mathieu et Georges Brassens voisinent avec des hommes d'Etat comme Charles de Gaulle. Une main ornée d'un cœur se dresse, en hommage à Coluche, dans le jardin réalisé entre 1963 et 1986. Favreau a construit une tombe pour Zappy, sa chienne bien-aimée, et une autre pour lui-même, de sorte qu'il repose en paix dans son univers. Des fresques – dont une dédiée aux victimes de Treblinka – et des reliefs tapissent l'intérieur de la maison. Une jeune femme nue, des papillons, des animaux terrestres et aquatiques décorent sa chambre.

Inside and outside, the house of Lucien Favreau is adorned with tableaux and sculptures. A sculpture of a young woman sits at the end of the bed, while a fresco of beauties looks down from the wall behind (following page).

Das Haus von Lucien Favreau ist außen und innen mit Gemälden und Skulpturen verziert. Am Fußende des Betts sitzt die Skulptur einer jungen Frau, das Fresko an der Rückwand zeigt weitere junge Mädchen (folgende Seite).

A l'extérieur et à l'intérieur, la maison de Lucien Favreau est ornée de bas-reliefs et de sculptures. La statue d'une femme assise se dresse au pied du lit, dominée par une frise de jeunes beautés (page suivante).

The animal sculptures are made of concrete inlaid with pieces of broken bottle.

Die Zementskulpturen sind mit Glasscherben bedeckt.

Les statues d'animaux sont en béton incrusté de morceaux de verre.

23

LaCasadel Cavaliere

Messina, Italy

Giovanni Cammarata (1914–2002), genannt »il Cavaliere« (der Ritter), besaß eine Fabrik für Gartendekorationen aus Zement. In seiner Freizeit legte er ab 1957 einen Skulpturengarten um sein Haus an, das in einem heruntergekommenen Viertel von Messina liegt. Die Außenwände des Gebäudes schmücken Zementreliefs mit historischen Szenen, darunter Hannibal mit seinen Elefanten und weitere antike Schlachten. Gerahmt werden die Reliefs von dekorativen Mustern aus Muscheln, Kieseln und Keramikstücken. Im Hof und im Garten befinden sich zahllose Skulpturen vor den reich verzierten Mauern: So stehen King Kong und Godzilla einträchtig neben Schneewittchen und den sieben Zwergen, sowie Heilige und Jungfrauen vor Tempeln, Kathedralen und Schlössern.

Giovanni Cammarata (1914–2002), or "il Cavaliere" (The Gentleman), had a business making cement garden ornaments, and his sculpture garden, started in 1957, was at first intended simply to display his talents. Situated in a run-down area of Messina, the house is covered in shells, pebbles and pottery fragments, forming decorative patterns around the cement reliefs of figures and animals. The latter include depictions of historical episodes, such as Hannibal and his elephants advancing on Italy. Within the decorated walls of his courtyard and garden stand scores of sculptures. Monsters like King Kong and Godzilla stand alongside Snow White and the Seven Dwarfs, while saints and Virgins pray beside temples, cathedrals and castles.

Entrepreneur, **Giovanni Cammarata** (1914–2002), dit «il Cavaliere» (Le Chevalier), fabriquait des ornements de jardin en ciment: à partir de 1957, il fit de sa maison, située dans un quartier délabré de Messine, une publicité grandeur nature. Sur les murs extérieurs, des coquillages, des galets et des tessons, entourent des bas-reliefs en béton représentant des personnages, des animaux et des scènes historiques, parmi lesquelles Hannibal et ses éléphants marchant sur l'Italie. Dans la cour et le jardin se presse une foule de sculptures sur fond de peintures murales et de mosaïques. King Kong et Godzilla voisinent avec Blanche-Neige et les Sept Nains, tandis que des madones et des saints se dressent devant des temples, des cathédrales ou des châteaux.

The encrusted walls of the crowded courtyard form a backdrop to reliefs and sculptures depicting beasts and events from classical history.

Darstellungen von verschiedenen Tieren und historischen Ereignissen bedecken die Mauern des gerade- zu überfüllten Innenhofes.

Les murs incrustés de la cour intérieure très décorée forment une toile de fond aux bas-reliefs et aux sculptures d'animaux et de scènes historiques.

27

IlCast elloin cantato

Sciacca, Italy

In the Twenties, **Filippo Bentivegna** (1888–1967) returned to his native Sicily from the United States after an unhappy love-affair. He devoted the rest of his life to creating a garden of hundreds of sculpted heads, carved from local stone and set into the walls and paths of the olive groves on his Sicilian smallholding. He lived as a hermit in a one-room hut, his Enchanted Castle, decorating the interior with murals and burrowing beneath it into caves, which he adorned with his sculpture. He refused to sell his work during his lifetime, though it is now represented at the Musée de l'Art Brut in Lausanne.

Nach einer gescheiterten Liebesbeziehung kehrte **Filippo Bentivegna** (1888–1967) in den zwanziger Jahren aus den Vereinigten Staaten in seine sizilianische Heimat zurück. Für den Rest seines Lebens widmete er sich der Bildhauerei und meißelte Hunderte von Köpfen in Steine, die aus der Umgebung stammen. Seine Werke stellte Bentivegna an den Mauern und Wegen seines Olivenhains oder in den Höhlen auf, die er unter seiner selbst ausgemalten Hütte, seinem »Zauberschloß«, aushob. Dort lebte er wie ein Einsiedler und weigerte sich, auch nur eines seiner Werke zu verkaufen. Erst nach seinem Tod wurden sie im Musée de l'Art Brut in Lausanne ausgestellt.

A la suite d'un amour malheureux, **Filippo Bentivegna** (1888–1967) quitta dans les années vingt les Etats-Unis pour revenir dans sa Sicile natale. Il consacra le reste de son existence à son jardin de têtes sculptées. Il en réalisa plusieurs centaines, taillées dans la pierre locale, qu'il disposa sur les murs et le long des sentiers sillonnant les oliveraies de sa petite terre. Vivant en ermite dans la pièce unique de sa cabane dite le «Château enchanté», il décora les murs de celle-ci et creusa en sous-sol des grottes qu'il orna de ses sculptures. Il a toujours refusé de vendre ses œuvres mais certaines ont rejoint, après sa mort, la collection du Musée de l'Art brut à Lausanne.

Hundreds of heads sculpted from local stone are laid out on the walls of the steep terraced hill, while others form the very fabric of the walls.

Auf dem terrassenartig angelegten Hanggelände sind Hunderte von Büsten aufgestellt, während weitere Skulpturen direkt in die Mauern eingelassen wurden. Die Steine beschaffte sich der Künstler in der Umgebung.

Des centaines de têtes sculptées dans la pierre locale couronnent les murets des terrasses; d'autres sont prises dans les murs mêmes.

La Cathédrale

Neuvy-Deux-Clochers, France

In 1961, ceramicist and potter **Jean Linard** (*1931) began erecting his "Cathedral" alongside the house he had built himself near Bourges. With its steeply angled roof, embellished with plant-holding gargoyles and monsters, the house evokes medieval architecture. The open air choir of the cathedral is flanked by the bright mosaic surfaces of angular structures and circular forms; tinkling globe mobiles are suspended from the trees. The choir is reached through an arched nave constructed from roughly hewn stone and supported by blue tiled buttresses. Various pyramidal structures, covered in ceramic and mirror mosaics, lead to the Baptistery, a large multi-coloured pyramid standing before a quiet contemplative pool. Linard makes all of his tiles himself, firing the clay in an open-air kiln and embedding them in the cement of his structures.

Im Jahr 1961 begann der Töpfer **Jean Linard** (*1931) mit dem Bau seiner »Kathedrale« in der Nähe von Bourges. Neben seinem selbst entworfenen Wohnhaus errichtete er ein mittelalterlich wirkendes Gebäude mit Erkern, Dachtürmen und Pflanzenkübeln in Form von Wasserspeiern und Fabelwesen. Von den Bäumen hängen klingende Mobiles. Der Chorraum liegt unter freiem Himmel und wird von schimmernden Mosaikwänden mit rechteckigen und runden Ornamenten gerahmt. Für das Mittelschiff verwendete Linard grob behauenen Stein und mit blauer Keramik verkleidete Stützpfeiler. Pyramidenförmige, mit Keramik- und Spiegelmosaiken geschmückte Bauten führen zur Taufkapelle, einer farbenprächtigen großen Pyramide mit einem Wasserbecken – eine Szenerie, die zur Kontemplation einlädt. Alle Keramiken brannte Linard in einem nahegelegenen Brennofen selbst und fügte sie in die Bauten ein.

Céramiste et potier, **Jean Linard** (*1931) a commencé à construire en 1961 sa Cathédrale à côté de la maison qu'il avait bâtie près de Bourges. L'habitation évoque le Moyen Age avec son toit pentu, ses gargouilles et ses jardinières en forme de monstres. Quant à la cathédrale, son chœur à ciel ouvert est entouré de structures géométriques et de formes circulaires couvertes de mosaïques aux couleurs vives; des mobiles qui tintent pendent aux arbres environnants. Le chœur se prolonge par une nef en pierres grossièrement taillées, soutenue par des contreforts carrelés de bleu. Plusieurs structures pyramidales, couvertes d'éclats de céramique et de miroir, mènent au Baptistère, grande pyramide bigarrée qui se reflète dans l'eau paisible d'un bassin. Linard a lui-même fabriqué les carreaux et les a cuits dans un four extérieur, puis les a incrustés dans les parois en ciment.

The steep angular structures are covered in colourful mosaics, while an array of gargoyles looks down from the roof of the house. Linard's self-built house stands alongside the Cathedral complex and forms an integral part of the visionary environment (following pages).

Ein farbenprächtiges Mosaik bedeckt die verwinkelten, hoch aufragenden Mauern. Das Dach zieren zahllose Wasserspeier. Das von Linard selbst errichtete Haus befindet sich neben der Kathedrale und fügt sich nahtlos in das Visionary Environment ein (folgende Doppelseite).

Des mosaïques chamarrées couvrent les édifices aux lignes élancées, tandis que des gargouilles peuplent le toit. Linard a construit sa Cathédrale dans le prolongement de sa maison qui fait donc partie intégrante de l'environnement visionnaire (double page suivante).

Cunégonde etMalabar

Nice, France

Ben Vautier (*1935) has been known as a conceptual artist since the Fifties, but now concentrates on graffiti, exhibiting graphic messages on canvas. Graffiti to him is a vehicle for not only cultural and political messages but also more personal poetic statements. He sees in graffiti a means of expression for those outside the normal cultural channels – minorities, women, children, and artists – all of whom are muzzled by the media and have no other outlet. He bought his house in Nice in 1976, and named it "Cunégonde and Malabar" after his children. Gradually it has filled up with a chaotic array of found objects set in a series of displays. The façade is festooned with objects, shop signs and Vautier's own graffito messages. A giant gnome stands before unfinished junk sculptures. Scores of old toilets and bidets act as plant containers and a giant rhinoceros-head stands guard above the doorway. Inside, amid Vautier's graffito pieces, painted ceilings and lively arrangements of kitsch objects, a space is reserved for the doll collection of his wife Annie.

Ben Vautier
(*1935) wurde in den fünfziger Jahren als Konzeptkünstler bekannt. Er wandte sich später Graffiti als Kunstform zur Übermittlung kultureller, politischer und persönlicher poetischer Botschaften zu und stellte Leinwand-Graffitis aus. Für Vautier ist Graffiti das einzig mögliche Sprachrohr derjenigen, die sich außerhalb der konventionellen Kulturkreise bewegen und die in den Medien wenig beachtet werden: Minderheiten, Frauen, Kinder und Künstler. 1976 erwarb Vautier ein Haus in Nizza und taufte es nach seinen Kindern »Cunégonde und Malabar«. Das Gebäude füllte sich nach und nach mit Fundstücken, die Vautier in verschiedenen Gruppen arrangierte. Diverse Objekte, Graffitis und Ladenschilder bedecken die Fassade. Im Vorgarten steht ein riesiger Gartenzwerg zwischen mehreren unvollendeten Trödelskulpturen sowie zahllosen ausgedienten Toilettenbecken und Bidets, die als Pflanzkübel dienen. Den Eingang bewacht ein gigantischer Rhinozeroskopf. Im Haus ist unter Deckengemälden neben Vautiers Graffitis und Kitsch-Objekten die Puppensammlung seiner Frau Annie ausgestellt.

Connu comme artiste conceptuel à partir des années cinquante, **Ben Vautier** (*1935) se tourne ensuite vers le graffiti et expose ses toiles. Pour lui, cet art convient à l'expression sociale et politique aussi bien que poétique et personnelle. C'est également, à ses yeux, un moyen de communication ouvert aux exclus des circuits culturels habituels – minorités, femmes, enfants ou artistes – muselés par les médias et privés d'exutoires. En 1976, Ben Vautier achète une maison à Nice et la nomme «Cunégonde et Malabar» d'après ses enfants. Peu à peu, il y accumule un véritable capharnaüm d'objets récupérés, qu'il dispose de différentes façons. Des enseignes, ses propres graffitis et diverses trouvailles envahissent la devanture. Des cuvettes de W.-C. et des bidets font office de pots de fleurs. Une grosse tête de rhinocéros monte la garde au-dessus de l'entrée. La collection de poupées d'Annie, la femme de l'artiste, des graffitis de Ben Vautier, des plafonds peints et des assemblages d'objets kitsch, composent le décor intérieur.

Ben has decorated the exterior of his house with found objects, for example a giant rhinoceros head, which he found in a flea market in Italy.

Ben hat die Außenwände seines Hauses mit Fundstücken dekoriert, wie zum Beispiel dem Rhinozeroskopf, der von einem italienischen Flohmarkt stammt.

Ben a décoré l'extérieur de sa maison avec des objets trouvés, par exemple la tête d'un rhinocéros provenant d'un marché aux puces, en Italie.

Ben places his treasures everywhere around the house, among them a giant garden gnome made by his friend Frédéric Roux. Various plants grow in old bidets around the garden. Ben indicates on the bathtub that, since 1917, the entire avant-garde is bathing in the dirty bath water of Marcel Duchamp. Ben's graffito messages are found even on his cement TV screen, which he thumps in disagreement.

Rund um das Haus finden sich Bens Schätze, darunter ein riesiger Gartenzwerg, das Werk seines Freundes Frédéric Roux. Pflanzen wachsen in den Bidetbecken im Garten. Auf die Badewanne hat Ben geschrieben, daß die gesamte Avantgarde seit 1917 in dem schmutzigen Badewasser von Marcel Duchamp badet. Sogar auf seinem Fernseher steht eine Botschaft. Ben schlägt gern auf den Zementbildschirm ein, wenn er mit dem Programm nicht einverstanden ist.

Ben a arrangé autour de la maison ses trésors, parmi lesquels se trouve un gros nain, l'œuvre de son ami Frédéric Roux. Ben a fait pousser des plantes dans des bidets blancs émaillés. Sur la baignoire, il a indiqué que, depuis 1917, toute l'avant-garde trempe dans l'eau de la baignoire de Marcel Duchamp. Même sur sa télévision dont l'écran est en ciment – pour taper dedans, quand il n'est pas d'accord – Ben a écrit son message.

Le Cy clop

Milly-la-Forêt, France

The Swiss sculptor **Jean Tinguely** (1925–1991) was a great admirer of the machines of Art Brut artist Anton Müller (1865–1930). Tinguely visited the Waldau asylum in Switzerland, where Müller had been a patient, to study documentation of Müller's machines, which sadly have not survived. Later, Tinguely used scrap materials and "objets trouvés" to create sculptures in a style all his own. In 1962, Tinguely met the artist **Niki de Saint Phalle** in Paris, and together they visited Ferdinand Cheval's Palais idéal (see pages 94–97), Antoni Gaudí's architectural masterpieces in Barcelona and, several years later, Simon Rodia's Watts Tower in Los Angeles (see pages 200–207). In 1969, without seeking permission from the French authorities, Tinguely and Niki de Saint Phalle erected Le Cyclop, a one-eyed cyclops head, in a woodland clearing at Milly-la-Forêt in the forest of Fontainebleau. Cybernetic and mechanical elements are integral parts of this iron sculpture on steel supports. Others shared in the creation of this monumental work of art: **Eva Aeppli, Daniel Spoerri** and **Bernhard Luginbühl**. Their contributions can be seen on the inside and outside of the head. This total artwork is a forerunner of the Tarot Garden in Tuscany (see pages 100–107), on which Saint Phalle has been working since 1979 with the aid of Tinguely.

Der Schweizer Bildhauer **Jean Tinguely** (1925–1991) begeisterte sich für die Maschinenkonstruktionen des Art-Brut-Künstlers Anton Müller (1865–1930). Er besuchte das Waldau-Sanatorium in der Schweiz, wo Anton Müller gelebt hatte, und studierte dort die Baupläne zu dessen Maschinen, die leider nicht erhalten sind. Später konstruierte Tinguely aus Altmaterialien und Fundobjekten eigene Skulpturen. Einige der Werke widmete er Anton Müller. 1962 lernte Tinguely in Paris die Künstlerin **Niki de Saint Phalle** kennen und besuchte mit ihr den Palais idéal von Ferdinand Cheval (siehe Seite 94–97), Antoni Gaudís architektonische Meisterwerke in Barcelona und einige Jahre später Watts Towers von Simon Rodia in Los Angeles (siehe Seite 200–207). Tinguely und Niki de Saint Phalle errichteten 1969 ohne behördliche Genehmigung in Milly-la-Forêt im Wald von Fontainebleau auf einer Lichtung einen einäugigen Zyklopenkopf. Kybernetische und mechanische Elemente sind organische Bestandteile der Eisenkonstruktion auf Stahlträgern. An der Großplastik waren unter anderem die Künstler **Eva Aeppli, Daniel Spoerri** und **Bernhard Luginbühl** beteiligt, deren Werke in die Gänge im Inneren und Äußeren des Kopfes eingefügt sind. Dieses Gesamtkunstwerk ging dem Tarotgarten (siehe Seite 100–107) voraus, den Saint Phalle ab 1979 mit Unterstützung von Tinguely in der Toskana errichtete.

Photo: Leonardo Bezzola

Fasciné par les étranges machines, aujourd'hui disparues, de Heinrich Anton Müller (1865–1930), **Jean Tinguely** (1925–1991) a étudié les croquis et les documents de l'artiste «art brut», conservés à l'hôpital psychiatrique de Waldau, en Suisse, où Müller avait été soigné. Par la suite, Tinguely utilisera des matériaux de récupération et des objets trouvés pour créer ses propres œuvres, au style si personnel. En 1962, il rencontre **Niki de Saint Phalle**. Ensemble, ils visitent le Palais idéal du facteur Cheval (voir pages 94–97), les chefs-d'œuvre de Gaudí à Barcelone et, des années plus tard, les Watts Towers de

Simon Rodia, à Los Angeles (voir pages 200–207). En 1969, sans avoir demandé les autorisations nécessaires, ils construisent dans une clairière de la forêt de Fontainebleau, à Milly-la-Forêt, leur célèbre Cyclop, sculpture métallique et mécanique reposant sur des supports en acier. **Eva Aeppli**, **Daniel Spoerri** et **Bernhard Luginbühl** participent à ce projet monumental, ornant l'intérieur et l'extérieur de la gigantesque tête. Cette œuvre totale est antérieure au Parc des Tarots (voir pages 100–107), créé en Toscane à partir de 1979 par Niki de Saint Phalle, avec l'aide de Tinguely.

Jean Tinguely's mechanical construction contrasts with the shimmering surfaces created by Niki de Saint Phalle.

Jean Tinguelys mechanische Konstruktionen heben sich von den schimmernden Oberflächen ab, die Niki de Saint Phalle gestaltet hat.

Les mécaniques de Jean Tinguely contrastent avec les structures miroitantes créées par Niki de Saint Phalle.

LaDe meure aux figur es

Dieulefit, France

Roland Dutel (*1955) is a former carpenter-builder who taught himself to paint and make assemblages, and has practised sculpture for the last 20 years. The transformation of his little farm in Dieulefit, near Valence, into a sculpture garden began in 1989, when he built a new gateway with pillars. Using reclaimed building materials from the local dump, recycled ceramics from local potteries, and other found materials, he and his partner Françoise covered the walls of his courtyard with moulded cement figures on a background of mosaic. The cellar beneath their house has been transformed into a rich labyrinth of grottoes. His house is open to visitors during the summer months.

Der ehemalige Tischlermeister **Roland Dutel** (*1955) hatte bereits 20 Jahre lang Skulpturen gestaltet, bevor er als Autodidakt an Gemälden und Assemblagen arbeitete. 1989 konstruierte er ein neues Tor für sein Landhaus in Dieulefit bei Valence. Gemeinsam mit seiner Partnerin Françoise legte Dutel das Mauerwerk im Hof mit Mosaiken und Figuren aus. Dabei verwendete er Keramikreste der örtlichen Töpferei, ausrangierte Werkstoffe der städtischen Mülldeponie und weitere Fundobjekte. Der Keller wurde zu einem verzweigten Labyrinth aus zahllosen Grotten. In den Sommermonaten kann das Haus besichtigt werden.

Peintre autodidacte, créateur d'assemblages, **Roland Dutel** (*1955) pratique la sculpture depuis 20 ans. Ancien charpentier, il commença en 1989 à transformer sa petite ferme de Dieulefit près de Valence, lorsqu'il refit le portail d'entrée, flanqué de piliers. Utilisant des matériaux de construction récupérés à la décharge du coin, auprès de faïenceries ou ailleurs, il recouvrit ensuite les murs de sa cour de mosaïques et de bas-reliefs en ciment moulé. Toujours avec l'aide de sa compagne, Françoise, il a fait de la cave un labyrinthe de grottes. On peut visiter l'endroit pendant les mois d'été.

The complex labyrinthine interior of Dutel's house, constructed of cement and plaster, is inlaid with glass, tiles and found objects.

Das komplexe, labyrinthische Innere von Roland Dutels Haus besteht aus Zement und Gips und wurde mit Glas, Ziegeln und Fundstücken verziert.

Le labyrinthe intérieur complexe de la maison de Roland Dutel, construite en ciment et plâtre, est décoré de verre, de tuiles et d'objets trouvés.

42

LaFer me-musée Barret

Sainte-Foy-la-Grande, France

Farmer **Franck Barret** was a medium and clairvoyant. From 1948, visions came to him at night, inspiring him to fill his house in Aquitaine with painted clay sculptures. Dominated by monsters and supernatural images, his works include a Yeti, Cro-Magnon Man, reptiles and saints. Barret claimed to have met a Martian, whom he immortalised in clay, while his visions of God the Father and Christ led to tableaux of holy figures, including the Holy Family, Christ surrounded by children, and the bearded, robed figure of God. The assembled figures and groups, often decked out in fur and feathers, have an eerie frozen quality.

Nächtliche Visionen inspirierten den Bauer **Franck Barret**, der auch Medium und Hellseher war, 1948 zum Bau eines ungewöhnlichen Hauses in Aquitanien, das er mit farbigen Lehmskulpturen füllte. Die meisten seiner Arbeiten stellen Ungeheuer und übernatürliche Wesen dar, darunter den Yeti, einen Steinzeitmenschen, Reptilien und verschiedene Heiligenfiguren. Die Skulptur eines Marsbewohners gestaltete Barret laut eigener Aussage nach einer tatsächlichen Begegnung. Gotteserscheinungen und Visionen von Jesus inspirierten ihn zu Darstellungen der Heiligen Familie, von Jesus inmitten von Kindern und Gott als bärtigem Mann in langem Gewand. Viele der Skulpturen, die mit Federn und Pelz geschmückt sind, hinterlassen beim Besucher einen beklemmenden Eindruck.

Franck Barret, agriculteur de son métier, était médium et voyant. Ses visions nocturnes lui inspirèrent à partir de 1948 la création des sculptures en argile peinte qui peuplent sa maison d'Aquitaine. Son œuvre grouille de monstres et d'évocations surnaturelles, au nombre desquelles un yéti, un homme de Cro-Magnon et des reptiles. Barret disait avoir rencontré un martien, dont il réalisa la sculpture en terre. Dieu et le Christ lui étant apparus, il composa des scènes représentant la Sainte Famille, le Christ entouré d'enfants, des saints, Dieu vêtu d'une grande robe et portant la barbe. Décors, personnages et créatures, souvent ornés de fourrure ou de plumes, ont un aspect figé, inquiétant.

Gillis à Barras

Saint-Front-sur-Lémance, France

Next to Charles de Gaulle stands the statue of an elderly man, presumably a self-portrait of Jean Prosper Gillis.

Neben Charles de Gaulle steht die Skulptur eines alten Mannes, in der Gillis sich vermutlich selber dargestellt hat.

La statue d'un hômme âgé, probablement un autoportrait de Gillis, se dresse à côté de celle du général de Gaulle.

Around the house near Bergerac, once occupied by **Jean Prosper Gillis** (1907–1974), animals of all shapes and sizes frolic in the grass – all of them made of brightly-painted cement. Between 1968 and 1973, the former bricklayer created his own Garden of Eden on a hillside plot, under the watchful eye of a statue of Charles de Gaulle. Standing close to the great man are an elephant, representing wisdom and strength, and a tiger, whose warlike nature symbolises the heroes of the Resistance. Further down the slope is an idyllic scene, in which dog and bear, kangaroo and zebra live peacefully side by side, and a boa-constrictor curls up contentedly next to a flamingo.

Rund um das Haus von **Jean Prosper Gillis** (1907–1974) bei Bergerac tummeln sich die verschiedensten Tiere im Gras, alle aus Zement geformt und bunt bemalt. Der ehemalige Maurer hat zwischen 1968 und 1973 auf einem Hanggrundstück einen »Garten Eden« geschaffen, der von der Statue von Charles de Gaulle bewacht wird.

Autour de la maison qu'occupait autrefois **Jean Prosper Gillis** (1907–1974), près de Bergerac, des animaux de toutes sortes, en ciment peint de couleurs vives, batifolent dans l'herbe. De 1968 à 1973, cet ancien maçon a créé son propre Eden sur un petit terrain à flanc de colline, surveillé par une statue de Charles de Gaulle. Près du grand homme se tiennent un éléphant, symbole de sagesse et de puissance, et un tigre dont le caractère guerrier évoque les héros de la Résistance. Plus bas, une scène idyllique représente un chien, un ours, un kangourou et un zèbre pacifiquement réunis, tandis qu'un boa constricteur, tranquillement lové, voisine avec un flamant rose.

Ihm zur Seite stehen ein Elefant als Verkörperung der Weisheit und Stärke sowie ein Tiger, der die kämpferische Natur des Résistance-Helden versinnbildlicht. Ihnen zu Füßen erstreckt sich eine friedliche Idylle, in der Hund und Bär, Känguruh und Zebra einträchtig nebeneinander stehen und sich eine Boa zufrieden neben einem Flamingo ringelt.

48

DasHaus derKünstler

Klosterneuburg-Gugging, Austria

Founded by Professor Leo Navratil in 1981, the Artists' House is a residential community of artist-patients from the psychiatric hospital at Klosterneuburg-Gugging near Vienna. The residents are encouraged to paint and draw as part of their daily lives. The artists, including **August Walla** (1936–2001), **Oswald Tschirtner** (*1920) and **Johann Garber** (*1947), have decorated the outside of the building with their powerful imagery and vibrant colours. There is also extensive decoration within the building. The Gugging artists continue with their work to this day and are represented in collections and museums throughout the world.

Das Haus der Künstler wurde 1981 von Professor Leo Navratil als Wohngemeinschaft von Künstler-Patienten der Niederösterreichischen Landesnervenklinik Klosterneuburg-Gugging bei Wien gegründet. Die Bewohner wurden ermutigt, Malen und Zeichnen in ihren Alltag zu integrieren. **August Walla** (1936–2001), **Oswald Tschirtner** (*1920) und **Johann Garber** (*1947) bemalten die Außenwände und Innenräume mit kraftvollen, starkfarbigen Bildern. Bis heute setzen die Künstler aus Gugging ihre Arbeit fort, und ihre Werke werden inzwischen weltweit in Sammlungen und Museen ausgestellt.

Fondée par le professeur Leo Navratil en 1981, la Maison des artistes accueille en résidence des patients artistes de la clinique neurologique de Klosterneuburg-Gugging, près de Vienne. Les pensionnaires, parmi lesquels **August Walla** (1936–2001), **Oswald Tschirtner** (*1920) et **Johann Garber** (*1947), pratiquent au quotidien la peinture et le dessin. Ils ont décoré d'œuvres puissantes aux couleurs exubérantes les murs extérieurs du bâtiment, ainsi qu'une grande partie de l'intérieur. Les artistes de Gugging continuent de créer des œuvres qui trouvent place dans des collections et des musées du monde entier.

Oswald Tschirtner's elongated figures contrast with the powerful colours of August Walla, who has completely covered his small room inside the building with paintings and emphatic messages and slogans (above and left).

Oswald Tschirtners langgestreckte Figuren kontrastieren mit August Wallas kräftigen Farben. Wallas Zimmer im Haus der Künstler ist ebenfalls mit Zeichnungen, eindringlichen Botschaften und Parolen dekoriert (oben und links).

Les personnages étirés d'Oswald Tschirtner contrastent avec les coloris puissants d'August Walla. Ce dernier a entièrement recouvert la petite chambre qu'il occupe de peintures et d'inscriptions véhémentes (ci-dessus et à gauche).

L'Héli ce terre stre

Saint-Georges-des-Sept-Voies, France

Jacques Warminski (1946–1996) has always had a strong interest in cave-dwellers and their habitats, visiting caves around the Mediterranean and the Middle East before, in 1987, purchasing an entire French troglodytic village that had been deserted by its inhabitants in the Fifties. Located near Angers, the village has now been transformed into his Terrestrial Helix, created between 1989 and 1993. Beneath the temple-like Amphi-Sculpture of swirling sculptural forms, the main caves, including over a kilometre of his own excavation, are approached by a spiralling slope leading to a dark passage that links a series of galleries. At the centre of the underground network is a cavity dominated by a large smooth sphere. The carved walls of the tunnels and caves match the convex forms created in the external landscape. Visitors explore the inside of the sculptures that they see on the surface and thus experience the unity of inner and outer worlds.

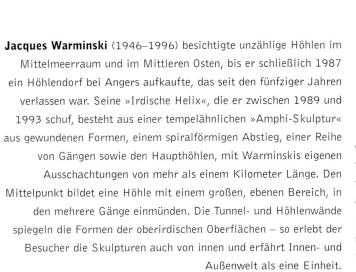

Jacques Warminski (1946–1996) besichtigte unzählige Höhlen im Mittelmeerraum und im Mittleren Osten, bis er schließlich 1987 ein Höhlendorf bei Angers aufkaufte, das seit den fünfziger Jahren verlassen war. Seine »Irdische Helix«, die er zwischen 1989 und 1993 schuf, besteht aus einer tempelähnlichen »Amphi-Skulptur« aus gewundenen Formen, einem spiralförmigen Abstieg, einer Reihe von Gängen sowie den Haupthöhlen, mit Warminskis eigenen Ausschachtungen von mehr als einem Kilometer Länge. Den Mittelpunkt bildet eine Höhle mit einem großen, ebenen Bereich, in den mehrere Gänge einmünden. Die Tunnel- und Höhlenwände spiegeln die Formen der oberirdischen Oberflächen – so erlebt der Besucher die Skulpturen auch von innen und erfährt Innen- und Außenwelt als eine Einheit.

Passionné par les habitats souterrains, dont il a visité bon nombre en Méditerranée et au Moyen-Orient, **Jacques Warminski** (1946–1996) a racheté un hameau troglodytique près d'Angers, abandonné depuis les années cinquante, et l'a transformé entre 1989 et 1993 en Hélice terrestre. Sous l'Amphi-Sculpture, sorte de vaste temple-théâtre en creux, se trouvent les grottes principales et plus d'un kilomètre de galeries, creusées par Warminski. On y accède par une déclivité en spirale plongeant dans un passage obscur. Au centre de cet univers souterrain se trouve une cavité dominée par une grande sphère lisse. Ornés de gravures, les tunnels et les grottes concaves correspondent en surface à autant de formes convexes, que les visiteurs découvrent avant d'y pénétrer: le monde extérieur et le monde intérieur sont ainsi indissolublement liés.

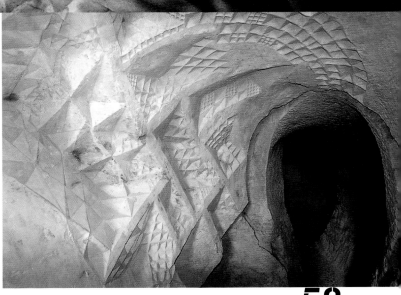

The flowing forms of the sculptures above the ground match the concave shapes in the caverns beneath.

Die fließende Gestaltung der Skulpturen auf der Erdoberfläche entspricht den konkaven Formen der darunterliegenden Höhlen.

Les sculptures arrondies et les formes concaves du sous-sol se font écho dans une parfaite unité.

LeJar dincoqu illage

Viry-Noureuil, France

Bodan Litnianski (1913–2005) emigrated to France from the Ukraine in the Thirties. Like many others, he found himself homeless after the Second World War. He bought a derelict house in Picardy for his family to live in, and restored it with reclaimed materials, using shells and glass fragments to decorate the walls. A former builder, cobbler and man-of-all-work, when he retired at the age of 62, he continued to embellish his house, building pillars densely packed with waste objects that had caught his eye. He collected dolls, bottles, mirrors, batteries, plastic toys, table football sets, televisions and toy animals and integrated them into his columns, which he fashioned of concrete around a framework of iron bars. The garden, surrounded by brightly decorated walls, became a labyrinth encrusted with fascinating objects, many of which have now acquired rarity value in their own right.

Bodan Litnianski (1913–2005) emigrierte in den dreißiger Jahren aus der Ukraine nach Frankreich. Im Zweiten Weltkrieg wurde er obdachlos und kaufte daraufhin in der Picardie ein heruntergekommenes Haus auf, das er mit allem restaurierte, was er finden konnte. So besserte er zum Beispiel die Wände mit Muscheln und Glasscherben aus. Litnianski arbeitete in verschiedenen Berufen, unter anderem als Steinmetz und Schuster. Als er sich mit 62 Jahren zur Ruhe setzte, widmete er sich der Arbeit an seinem Garten. Er errichtete Zementsäulen mit einem Eisengerüst und schmückte sie mit ausgedienten Puppen, Flaschen, Spiegeln, Batterien, Plastikspielzeug, Tischfußballspielen, Fernsehern und Stofftieren. Im Lauf der Jahre entstand ein mit bemalten Mauern umgebenes Labyrinth aus faszinierenden Objekten.

Bodan Litnianski (1913–2005) quitte l'Ukraine pour la France dans les années trente. Comme beaucoup d'autres après la Seconde Guerre mondiale, il se retrouve sans toit. Il achète alors en Picardie une maison en ruine qu'il réaménage avec des matériaux de récupération; il incruste dans les murs des coquillages et des débris de verre. Il exerce différents métiers, maçon, cordonnier et homme à tout faire, puis prend sa retraite à 62 ans et décide de construire autour de sa maison des empilements d'objets de récupération. Il déniche des poupées, des miroirs, des piles, des jouets et des animaux en plastique, des baby-foot, des postes de télévision, et les intègre à de grandes colonnes, formées de barres de fer recouvertes de béton. Il érige peu à peu un labyrinthe de palissades, entouré de murs aux couleurs vives. Au fil des ans, les objets étonnants qui le composent sont devenus de véritables raretés.

Bodan Litnianski topped one of his closely packed constructions with an aeroplane built by his son.

Bodan Litnianski krönte eine seiner kompakten Konstruktionen mit einem von seinem Sohn gebauten Flugzeug.

Bodan Litnianski a couronné d'un avion construit par son fils l'une de ses pyramides foisonnantes.

LeJar din deNo usDeux

Civrieux-d'Azergues, France

Nachdem der Miederwarenfabrikant **Charles Billy** (1910–1991) sich zur Ruhe gesetzt hatte, errichtete er ab 1975 bei seinem Haus am Stadtrand von Lyon mehrere mittelalterlich und orientalisch wirkende Bauten. In den Ruinen von Bauernhöfen der Umgebung fand er goldfarbenen Sandstein, den er nach mittelalterlicher Bautechnik über hölzernen Lehrgerüsten zu Bögen und Gewölben verbaute. Reliefs, Figurinen, Schnitzereien und Geheimsymbole schmücken die Bauten, die durch gewundene Pfade miteinander verbunden sind. Ein farbenprächtiger Garten umgibt das mystische Meisterwerk aus unzähligen Kuppeln, Türmen, Gewölben und Bögen, das Billy als »Unser beider Garten« sich und seiner Frau Pauline widmete. Eine Treppe mit 14 in Stein gehauenen Stufen führt zu einem orientalischen Tempel auf den oberen Terrassen, den Elefanten und Tänzer als Relief zieren. Billy legte hinter dem Haus eine Terrasse mit aufwendigen Mosaikarbeiten an, wo er gerne saß, um sein Werk zu betrachten. Inspiriert hatte ihn wohl ein Besuch des Palais idéal von Ferdinand Cheval (siehe Seite 94–97), aber Billy behauptete, sein komplexes Werk schon im Mittelalter begonnen und jetzt nach 500jährigem Schlaf nur vollendet zu haben.

After a career as a corset maker, **Charles Billy** (1910–1991) devoted his retirement to creating a mass of oriental and medieval-style buildings around his trim house near Lyon. Using golden sandstone reclaimed from ruined rural buildings, he employed traditional methods of construction, building arches and vaults on meticulously constructed wooden supports. He embellished his creation with reliefs, figurines, carvings and arcane imagery. Connected by winding paths, and surrounded by dense foliage and colourful flowers, his monumental creation is a masterpiece of domes, turrets, vaults and arches. Begun in 1975, it is a proud tribute to himself and his wife Pauline; he named it the "Garden of the Two of Us". The upper terraces are reached by 14 engraved steps that lead to an oriental temple with reliefs of elephants and dancers. Around his house he laid a complex mosaic terrace, where he could sit and admire the vistas that he had created. He had visited the Palais idéal of the Facteur Cheval (see pages 94–97) and may well have found in it the inspiration for his own architectural extravaganza. Billy claimed to have begun his complex in the Middle Ages, only to be overcome by sleep; awakening 500 years later, he set about completing it.

Fabricant de gaines et de soutiens-gorge, **Charles Billy** (1910–1991) consacra sa retraite à la réalisation d'un ensemble architectural de style oriental et médiéval, bâti à partir de 1975 autour de sa coquette maison des faubourgs de Lyon. Il utilisa des techniques de construction traditionnelles, édifiant sur des supports en bois méticuleusement conçus des arcs et des voûtes en pierres dorées, récupérées dans des ruines de la campagne alentour. Il orna ses édifices de sculptures et de statues, de figurines et de représentations ésotériques. Reliées par des chemins sinueux, entourées d'un foisonnement de plantes et de fleurs, ses extraordinaires compositions monumentales ponctuées d'innombrables tourelles se voulaient aussi un hommage au couple qu'il formait avec sa femme Pauline. 14 marches sculptées mènent aux terrasses supérieures et à un temple oriental orné de reliefs d'éléphants et de danseurs. Près de la maison, une terrasse tapissée de mosaïques permettait au maître des lieux de contempler son œuvre. Billy avait visité le Palais idéal du facteur Cheval (voir pages 94–97), dont il s'inspira peut-être pour créer son chef-d'œuvre d'architecture mystique. Il disait avoir entrepris ces travaux au Moyen Age puis les avoir repris au 19e siècle, après un long sommeil de 500 ans.

Small reliefs and tableaux of humorous scenes adorn the fantasy of Charles Billy which incorporates architectural influences from all around the world. Bridges, windmills, spires and courtyards were all constructed in the medieval style.

Die Phantasiewelt von Charles Billy zeigt architektonische Einflüsse aus der ganzen Welt. Humoristische Szenen schmücken als Reliefs und Tableaux die Gebäude, darunter Brücken, Windmühlen, Türme und Innenhöfe im mittelalterlichen Stil.

De petits bas-reliefs et des scènes pleines d'humour ornent les architectures fantastiques de Charles Billy, inspirées d'édifices du monde entier. Ponts, moulins à vent, tourelles et cours, bâtis avec un soin extrême, créent un décor de style médiéval.

Jar dinscul pté Gabriel

Brizambourg, France

Albert Gabriel (1904–1999) always wanted to be a sculptor, but force of circumstance led him to earn his living as a manual worker; he was able to realise his ambition only on retirement in 1967. His sculpture garden, near Cognac, consists of hundreds of busts and full-length figures, constructed of coloured cement over metal frames; they represent many of the public and popular personalities of his time. French Presidents Jacques Chirac, François Mitterrand and Valéry Giscard d'Estaing are all present, as are entertainers Charlie Chaplin, Georges Brassens and Jacques Brel. His garden also displays angels, representatives of foreign peoples and a series of seductive bare-breasted dancing beauties.

Albert Gabriel's depictions of local people stand alongside famous personalities of our time such as Charlie Chaplin and General de Gaulle.

Albert Gabriels Skulpturen umfassen Lokalgrößen ebenso wie berühmte Persönlichkeiten wie Charlie Chaplin oder Charles de Gaulle.

Parmi les nombreux personnages d'Albert Gabriel, on croise des gens de tous les jours auxquels se mêlent des personnages comme Charlie Chaplin et Charles de Gaulle, entre autres.

Albert Gabriel (1904–1999) wollte immer schon Bildhauer werden, doch die Umstände zwangen ihn, seinen Lebensunterhalt mit Schwerstarbeit zu verdienen. Erst als Rentner verwirklichte er seinen Lebenstraum und legte ab 1967 bei Cognac einen Garten mit Skulpturen an, die er aus Zement über einer Metallkonstruktion formte und bemalte. In Hunderten von Büsten und lebensgroßen Statuen sind bekannte Persönlichkeiten festgehalten: die französischen Präsidenten Jacques Chirac, François Mitterrand und Valéry Giscard d'Estaing, aber auch Charlie Chaplin, Georges Brassens und Jacques Brel. Und schließlich fanden Engel, Menschen verschiedenster Nationalitäten und verführerische barbusige Tänzerinnen einen Platz in Gabriels Garten.

Tout jeune, **Albert Gabriel** (1904–1999) rêvait de devenir sculpteur mais il lui fallut gagner sa vie comme ouvrier et attendre la retraite en 1967 pour se consacrer à sa passion. Situé dans les Charentes, son jardin sculpté abrite des centaines de bustes et de personnages en pied, réalisés à partir de structures en métal recouvertes de ciment coloré. On y croise de nombreuses personnalités de notre époque, comme les présidents français Jacques Chirac, François Mitterrand et Valéry Giscard d'Estaing, ou des gens du spectacle tels Charlie Chaplin, Georges Brassens et Jacques Brel. Sans compter des anges, quantité de personnages anonymes et de belles danseuses aux seins nus.

LeJardin zoologique

Thorée-les-Pins, France

Die künstlerische Leidenschaft von **Emile Taugourdeau** (1917–1989) erwachte, als 1974 seine Ente starb und er sie in einer Plastik verewigte. Im Lauf der Jahre gestaltete der ehemalige Steinmetz einen kompletten Zoo, aber er nahm in seinen Tierpark bei Tours auch Menschen auf: ein Brautpaar, einen Mofafahrer, Fußballer, Polizisten und kleine Kinder. Am Garteneingang begrüßt eine indianische Göttin mit zwei riesigen Schlangen neben einer Windmühle und Zementbäumen die Besucher. Der Künstler war bekannt für seine schnelle Arbeitsweise und bemalte den noch feuchten Zement, der die Farbe aufsog. Seit Taugourdeaus Tod kümmert sich seine Frau Denise um den Garten.

A la mort de son canard, en 1974, **Emile Taugourdeau** (1917–1989) décida d'immortaliser son compagnon: cette première statue donna naissance à une véritable passion et, peu à peu, à un zoo entier près de Tours. Des personnages humains firent leur apparition: un couple de jeunes mariés, un charretier, des footballeurs, des gendarmes et de petits enfants. A l'entrée, à côté d'un moulin et d'arbres en ciment, une déesse indienne, autour de laquelle s'enroulent deux énormes serpents, accueille les visiteurs. Ancien maçon, Taugourdeau travaillait vite, peignant le ciment encore humide afin qu'il absorbe mieux la couleur. Depuis sa mort, le jardin est entretenu par sa femme Denise.

When his duck died in 1974, **Emile Taugourdeau** (1917–1989) decided to immortalise it by sculpting in cement. The resulting statue inaugurated a creative passion that grew over the years into a Zoological Garden full of birds and beasts. The former builder also included human figures, with a bride and groom, a cart-driver, footballers, gendarmes and small children. At the entrance visitors are greeted by an Indian goddess draped with two huge snakes, standing alongside a cement windmill and cement trees. He worked quickly, painting the damp cement so that it would absorb the colour. Since his death the garden near Tours has been tended by his wife Denise.

Emile Taugourdeau created the figures and animals of his Zoological Garden to please his children. When it is sunny, the colours of the sculptures can be seen properly, many of them a rain-soaked moss green. The sculptures have not been repainted since Taugourdeau died.

Emile Taugourdeau schuf die Gestalten und Tiere in seinem Zoologischen Garten, um seine Kinder zu erfreuen. Wenn die Sonne scheint, leuchtet das Moos auf den farbig bemalten Skulpturen, denn seit dem Tod von Taugourdeau ist die Farbe nicht mehr erneuert worden.

Taugourdeau a imaginé les animaux et les personnages de son zoo pour amuser ses enfants. Les sculptures n'ont pas été repeintes depuis sa mort et la mousse les recouvre peu à peu mais, par beau temps, les couleurs reprennent toute leur vigueur.

63

DasJ unker haus

Lemgo, Germany

Architecture, woodcarving and painting are uniquely combined in the house begun in 1889/1890 by the artist and former cabinet-maker **Karl Junker** (1850–1912) at Lemgo near Bielefeld. Some years before, he had returned from Italy where he spent two years after winning a travelling scholarship from the Munich Academy of Fine Arts. Until his death, Junker led a solitary life, devoting himself to working on his house, which he decorated with thousands of different images. Countless figurative and ornamental reliefs, embracing couples and Christian symbols in wood form a closely-woven network covering the external walls, panelling, floorboards, ceiling and even the stairs. Junker used fine brush strokes to accentuate details, framing colourful scenes with medallions. He painted the external walls in shades of red, yellow and blue. The furniture, decorated with extravagant carvings which seem to lead a life of their own, was also Junker's own work. Junker's legacy includes innumerable paintings, drawings, gouaches and sculptures, now languishing in the storeroom of the local museum.

A Lemgo, près de Bielefeld, **Karl Junker** (1850–1912), artiste et ébéniste, a construit à partir des années 1889/1890 une maison étonnante où l'architecture le dispute à la sculpture sur bois et à la peinture. Après un séjour de deux ans en Italie, grâce à une bourse qu'il avait obtenue sur concours auprès de l'académie des beaux-arts de Munich, il s'installa dans cette maison qu'il décora de milliers d'œuvres. Il y vécut en solitaire jusqu'à la fin de sa vie. Les bas-reliefs en bois, décoratifs ou figuratifs, des couples enlacés et des symboles chrétiens, forment un entrelacs qui recouvre les murs extérieurs, les boiseries, les planchers, les plafonds et même l'escalier. Junker a souligné les détails de petites touches de peinture et encadré de médaillons des scènes pleines de couleurs. Dehors, les murs s'ornent de motifs rouges, jaunes et bleus. Le maître des lieux a également construit les meubles, décorés de sculptures extravagantes qui semblent animées d'une vie propre. Junker a laissé d'innombrables peintures, dessins et sculptures, relégués aujourd'hui dans la réserve du musée local.

The carved ornamentation of the Junkerhaus owes much to the local style known as "Weserrenaissance".

Die geschnitzten Verzierungen des Junkerhauses sind stilistisch der Weserrenaissance verwandt.

Le décor sculpté du Junkerhaus doit beaucoup à un style régional, le style «Weserrenaissance».

Architektur, Holzbildhauerei und Malerei bilden eine ungewöhnliche Einheit in dem Wohnhaus, das der Künstler und ehemalige Kunsttischler **Karl Junker** (1850–1912) ab 1889/1890 in Lemgo bei Bielefeld errichtete. Er war einige Jahre zuvor von einem zweijährigen Italienaufenthalt zurückgekehrt, nachdem er den Rompreis der Münchener Akademie der Schönen Künste gewonnen hatte. Bis zu seinem Tod führte Junker ein zurückgezogenes Leben, lebte nur für die Arbeit an seinem Haus und verzierte es mit Tausenden von geschnitzten Profilleisten. Unzählige figürliche und ornamentale Holzreliefs, einander umarmende Paare, christliche Motive oder einfach nur Buckel oder Knorpel überziehen wie ein engmaschiges Netz Außenwände, Vertäfelungen, Bodendielen, Decke und sogar die Treppenstufen. Mit feinen Pinselstrichen akzentuierte Junker Details, fügte in Medaillons farbenfrohe Szenen ein und bemalte die Außenwände in Rot-, Gelb- und Blautönen. Auch die Möbel fertigte er selber an und verzierte sie ebenfalls mit überbordenden Schnitzereien, die ein Eigenleben zu führen scheinen. Junkers Nachlaß umfaßt außerdem unzählige Gemälde, Zeichnungen, Gouachen und Plastiken, die sich heute im Magazin des Städtischen Museums befinden.

The drawing room is on the first floor. Karl Junker built the upholstered furniture and bureau. In the ground-floor workshop (facing page) is a chest carved with the figure of Christ in the Tomb.

Der sogenannte Salon befindet sich im ersten Stock. Auch die Polstermöbel und den Sekretär hat Karl Junker selber angefertigt. Im Atelier im Erdgeschoß (rechte Seite) steht eine Truhe mit dem geschnitzten Leichnam Christi.

Le séjour se trouve au premier étage. Junker a construit les meubles tapissés et le bureau. Dans l'atelier du rez-de-chaussée (page de droite), la figure du Christ au tombeau repose sur une malle sculptée.

TheLittleChapel

St. Andrew, Guernsey, England

Frère Déodat (1878–1951) kam 1913 als Lehrer an eine Klosterschule nach Guernsey. Nach dem Vorbild von Lourdes errichtete er hier 1914 eine winzige Kapelle und später ein Gebäude von sechs Quadratmetern Größe. An seiner Stelle entstand die Little Chapel, weil der beleibte Bischof von Portsmouth das Bauwerk nicht betreten konnte. 1923 begannen die Arbeiten an einer doppelt so großen Kapelle. Der Rohbau war zwei Jahre später fertiggestellt und wurde mit Kieselglas und Keramikstücken dekoriert. Aus der ganzen Welt wurden Déodat weitere Dekorationsstücke geschickt, darunter eine eindrucksvolle Perlmutter, die er vom Vizegouverneur der Insel erhielt.

Frère Déodat (1878–1951) arrived in Guernsey in 1913; he belonged to a monastic order devoted to the education of boys. Inspired by the grotto at Lourdes, he built a grotto, and then his tiny "first chapel" in 1914. This he replaced with another 9 foot long by 6 foot wide. The portly Bishop of Portsmouth was unable to enter, so in 1923 Déodat destroyed his second effort and began work on the present chapel, which is double the size. It took two years to build the basic structure, whose surfaces Déodat then decorated with pebbles and broken crockery. Déodat received decorative pieces from all over the world,

including a huge piece of mother of pearl from the island's Lieutenant-Governor.

Appartenant à un ordre religieux voué à l'éducation des garçons, le **Frère Déodat** (1878–1951) arriva à Guernesey en 1913. Il s'inspira de Lourdes pour bâtir une grotte puis une première petite chapelle, en 1914. Il remplaça cette dernière par une autre, mesurant trois mètres sur deux. Le corpulent évêque de Portsmouth n'ayant pu y pénétrer, Déodat la détruisit et entreprit en 1923 de construire la chapelle actuelle, en doublant les dimensions. Il lui fallut deux ans pour édifier la structure de base, dont il décora ensuite les surfaces avec des galets et de la vaisselle cassée. Il reçut des éléments décoratifs envoyés du monde entier, y compris un énorme morceau de nacre offert par le lieutenant-gouverneur de l'île.

Inside and out, the chapel is encrusted with countless pebbles, shells, broken crockery and donated materials.

Die Innen- und Außenwände sind mit zahllosen Kieselsteinen, Muscheln, Keramikscherben und geschenkten Dekorationsstücken bedeckt.

Galets, coquillages, céramique et matériaux décoratifs offerts au Frère Déodat recouvrent entièrement les parois, dehors comme dedans.

La Maison à la vaisselle cassée

Louviers, France

Im Jahr 1952 begannen der ehemalige Milchwagenfahrer **Robert Vasseur** (1908–2002) und seine Frau, ihr Haus bei Rouen und den Garten mit Keramikscherben und Muscheln zu verzieren. An der Fassade verweist ein großer Schmetterling inmitten schimmernder Mosaiken auf den CB-Funk-Codenamen von Vasseur: Schmetterling 27. Im Innenhof setzen sich die Mosaiken über verschiedene Bauten fort: eine mit Muscheln belegte Hundehütte, ein aufwendiger Springbrunnen, der sich mit dem fließenden Wasser dreht, und ein mosaikbedeckter Kohleschuppen. Das Innere des »Scherbenhauses« ist ebenfalls reich geschmückt. Hier befindet sich auch das alte Zementspülbecken, der erste Gegenstand, den das Paar mit Mosaiken auslegte. Vasseur hatte eine Vereinbarung mit der örtlichen Mülldeponie getroffen, die für ihn Keramikscherben sammelte. Bevor er die Stücke verwendete, reinigte und sterilisierte er sie sorgfältig.

Robert Vasseur (1908–2002), a former milk-delivery driver, started in 1952 to decorate his house and garden near Rouen with shells and broken crockery, aided throughout by his wife. The exterior walls of the house shimmer with decorative imagery. They are dominated by a huge butterfly, which refers to Vasseur's CB radio code name, Butterfly 27. Within the courtyard, the mosaic surfaces cover a variety of structures, including a dog kennel encrusted with shells, and a complex fountain, which is rotated by the flow of its waters. Even the coalshed has been encased in mosaic. The interior of the House of Broken Crockery is also encrusted with decoration; one can still see the first object to receive mosaic treatment, an old cement sink. Vasseur had an arrangement with the local dump to put aside broken crockery for him to collect, each piece of which he carefully washed and sterilised.

Robert Vasseur (1908–2002), livreur de lait de son métier, et sa femme ont commencé en 1952 à décorer leur maison et leur jardin près de Rouen, avec de la vaisselle cassée et des coquillages. Les murs extérieurs chatoient sous les ornements, parmi lesquels se détache un immense papillon, allusion au nom de code «Papillon 27» utilisé par Vasseur sur les ondes de la C.B. Dans la cour, des sols en mosaïque longent différents édicules, dont une niche ornée de coquillages et une fontaine tournante actionnée par le mouvement de l'eau. Même la cabane à charbon disparaît sous les incrustations, tout comme l'intérieur de la demeure et le premier objet ainsi traité, un vieil évier en ciment. Vasseur s'était entendu avec un éboueur qui lui mettait de côté la vaisselle cassée; il lavait et désinfectait ensuite chaque débris.

70

71

Robert Vasseur's garden is a mass of mosaic and decorated forms. There are several whirligigs, a fountain with moving parts, and even the coal shed is as richly adorned as the dog's kennel. Inside, some of the walls and ceilings of the house are similarly ornate.

Robert Vasseurs Scherbenhaus ist mit zahllosen Mosaiken und weiterem Dekor bedeckt. Zu der Anlage gehören verschiedene Karussells, ein Springbrunnen aus beweglichen Elementen, ein reich verzierter Kohleschuppen sowie eine Hundehütte. Einige Innenwände und Zimmerdecken des Gebäudes sind kunstvoll verziert.

Mosaïques et ornements envahissent le jardin de Robert Vasseur, recouvrant plusieurs tourniquets éoliens, une fontaine animée, la cabane à charbon et même la niche du chien. Dans la maison, plusieurs plafonds et murs sont également décorés.

LaMaison deCelle-peint

Pont-de-l'Etoile, France

Danielle Jacqui (*1934), dite «Celle-qui-peint», commença dans les années soixante-dix à faire de la broderie pour attirer des clients sur son stand de foire. Elle a mis un an à composer sa première œuvre, une broderie compliquée aux couleurs vives. Elle aborde ensuite la peinture et la réalisation d'objets et de personnages brodés. Peu à peu, son élan créateur envahit sa maison et son existence. Dans sa demeure, les surfaces se couvrent rapidement de mosaïques somptueuses en tessons de céramiques et de miroirs, combinées avec des peintures proliférantes. Les formes se fondent les unes dans les autres, noyant les limites entre les murs et le plafond. L'abondance des matières et des couleurs captive le regard. La façade de la petite maison près de Marseille s'orne de tableaux suspendus et d'un bas-relief en mosaïque qui ne cesse de s'étendre. Danielle Jacqui est un membre éminent des Artistes singuliers, groupe d'artistes autodidactes de Provence.

Danielle Jacqui (*1934), known as "She Who Paints", started embroidery to attract customers while working in fleamarkets. Her first creation, in the Seventies, was a complex, brightly coloured embroidery that took over a year to finish. From this she progressed to painting, making three-dimensional objects and embroidery figures. Gradually her creative urge took over her life – and her house. Before long, its interior surfaces were covered with a rich colourful mosaic of mirror and ceramic fragments, combined with richly painted images. Overpowering in texture and colour, the continually evolving forms flow one into another around the house, heedless of the distinction between wall and ceiling. The paintings attached to the facade of this little village house near Marseille now have as their background an ever-growing mosaic relief. Danielle Jacqui is one of the foremost members of the Artistes Singuliers group of self-taught artists from Provence in southern France.

Danielle Jacqui (*1934), bekannt als »Die Malende«, begann in den siebziger Jahren, aufwendige und farbenfrohe Stickereien anzufertigen, um auf Flohmärkten Kundschaft anzuziehen. An der ersten Stickerei arbeitete sie über ein Jahr. Dann fing sie an zu malen, gestaltete dreidimensionale Objekte und stickte Figuren. Ihr Leben wurde mehr und mehr von ihrer Kunst beherrscht, und die Innenwände ihres Hauses bedeckten sich mit farbenfrohen Mosaiken aus Spiegel- und Keramikscherben sowie Malereien. Die verwirrenden Farben und Strukturen ließen fließende Übergänge zwischen Wänden und Zimmerdecken entstehen. Die Fassade des Häuschens bei Marseille schmücken Gemälde und ein stetig wachsendes Mosaikrelief. Inzwischen ist Danielle Jacqui eines der bekanntesten Mitglieder der Artistes singuliers, einer Gruppe autodidaktischer Künstler aus der Provence.

The outside of the house is festooned with paintings, while the staircase has become a work of art in its own right. Every inch of Jacqui's house is covered with mosaic, paint and assemblages.

Das Haus von Danielle Jacqui ist bunt bemalt. Jeder Zentimeter ihres Domizils ist mit Mosaiken, Farbe und Assemblagen bedeckt, und selbst die Treppe wirkt wie eine drei-dimensionale Leinwand.

La maison de Danielle Jacqui est peinte de couleurs vives. Le moindre centimètre carré est recouvert de mosaïques, de peinture ou d'assemblages; même l'escalier évoque une toile tridimensionnelle.

mon carré de pissenlit
larme bleue, bleue
bleu sérénité
cautérise calme
danielle jacqui

Jacqui's paintings – here details of her works "Sea-scape" (La Marine) and "War" (La Guerre) – are thickly textured, echoing their creative origins in embroidery. She also has created dolls, for example "Julie", and makes her own clothes, becoming a walking work of art. The portrait shows her with the dress "Scarlett O'Hara" made of green velvet.

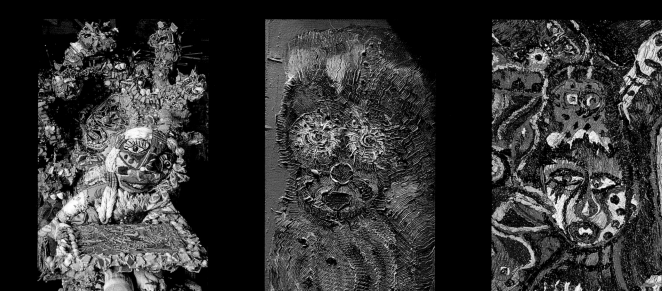

Die dick aufgetragenen Farben in den Gemälden verraten, daß Danielle Jacqui ursprünglich Stickereien fertigte. Die Details zeigen Ausschnitte aus ihren Arbeiten »Seestück« (La Marine) und »Der Krieg« (La Guerre) sowie ihre Puppe »Julie«. Danielle Jacqui gestaltet auch ihre eigene Kleidung und wird so zum lebenden Kunstwerk: hier sieht man sie in dem grünen Samtkleid »Scarlett O'Hara«.

Les couleurs largement étalées révèlent que Danielle Jacqui réalisait initialement des broderies. Les détails montrent des extraits de ses travaux «La Marine» et «La Guerre» ainsi que la poupée «Julie». Danielle Jacqui conçoit aussi ses vêtements et devient ainsi une œuvre d'art vivante. Elle porte ici la robe de velours vert «Scarlett O'Hara».

La Mais on Pic assiette

Chartres, France

Photo: Michel Boudaud

Raymond Isidore (1904–1964) was a humble cemetery sweeper in Chartres, an occupation that gave him little satisfaction. Starting in 1937, after each working day, he collected fragments of glass and pottery, using them to decorate the little house he had built for his wife and himself. Eventually the whole interior of the building, including furniture, was coated in mosaics. He then began work on his garden, creating a series of intimate courtyards covered in shimmering ornaments and images, even constructing potted "plants" in mosaic. The culmination of his creative powers is the final series of courtyards, with standing figures and shrines leading to a magnificent throne. The religious impact of Chartres is evident in his depictions of the city of Jerusalem and of great cathedrals, and in the tomb topped by a model of Chartres cathedral itself. His pictorial references were postcards, newspaper photographs, and calendars. Isidore became known as "Picassiette", a play on "Picasso" and "assiette", also spelt "pique-assiette" (plate-scrounger). A visit to this place, well maintained by the municipality, is an overwhelming experience.

Raymond Isidore (1904–1964) war Friedhofswächter; in seiner Freizeit dekorierte er ab 1937 mit Glas- und Tonscherben das kleine Haus in Chartres, das er für sich und seine Frau errichtet hatte, bis alle Innenräume, einschließlich der Möbel, mit Mosaiken bedeckt waren. Er setzte die Arbeit im Garten fort und gestaltete eine Reihe kleiner Höfe, über und über bedeckt mit glitzernden Ornamenten und sogar Pflanzenmosaiken. Auf dem Höhepunkt seiner Kreativität schuf Isidore mehrere Statuen und Schreine, die zu einem prächtigen Thron führen. Der religiöse Einfluß zeigt sich in Bildern von Jerusalem und großen Kathedralen einschließlich derjenigen von Chartres. Als Vorlage dienten Postkarten, Zeitungs- und Kalenderbilder. Bekannt wurde Isidore unter dem Pseudonym »Picassiette« – ein Wortspiel aus »Picasso« und »assiette« (Teller). Mit anderer Betonung kann es auch auch als »pique-assiette« (Schnorrer) verstanden werden. Die Stadt Chartres ist sehr um die Erhaltung dieses Bauwerkes bemüht, und so ist ein Besuch in der Welt des Raymond Isidore nach wie vor ein überwältigendes Erlebnis.

Raymond Isidore (1904–1964) était balayeur dans un cimetière près de Chartres, un travail qu'il n'aimait pas. A partir de 1937, une fois sa journée finie, il récupérait des débris de verre et de vaisselle cassée et se consacrait à la décoration de la petite maison qu'il avait construite et où il vivait avec sa femme. Lorsque tout l'intérieur, meubles compris, fut recouvert de mosaïques incrustées dans du ciment coloré, il entreprit de créer dans le jardin une série de courettes secrètes, décorées dans leurs moindres recoins; les mosaïques dessinaient même des plantes en pot. Couronnement de son œuvre, les derniers enclos abritaient des figures en pied et des châsses ainsi qu'un superbe trône. Pour y représenter Jérusalem et de grandes églises, Isidore s'inspira de la cathédrale de Chartres, dont la reproduction domine l'ensemble. Il travaillait à partir de cartes postales, de journaux illustrés et de calendriers. Créateur d'un environnement visionnaire comptant aujourd'hui parmi les grands classiques du genre, il devint célèbre sous le nom de «Picassiette» – contraction de «Picasso» et d'«assiette» – ou de «pique-assiette». Son univers, placé sous la garde vigilante de la municipalité, est à visiter.

Raymond Isidore covered every surface in his house with mosaic and decoration, including all the furniture, the kitchen range and the radio.

Raymond Isidore bedeckte alle Oberflächen seines Hauses, sogar die Möbel, die Kücheneinrichtung und das Radio, mit Mosaiken und anderem Schmuck.

Raymond Isidore a recouvert de mosaïques et de décorations toute sa maison, y compris les meubles, le fourneau et même la radio.

LeMa nège

Dicy, France

Pierre Avezard (1909–1992), known as "Petit Pierre", was a cowherd with a penchant for complex mechanical construction. Between 1937 and 1974, he built a Merry-go-round beside his isolated house in Fay-aux-Loges near Orléans. It was a buzzing automated delight, comprising trains, buses, aeroplanes and trams, complete with human and animal passengers, whirling around on various tracks and wires. Controlled by home-made signal boxes made of old nails and air-chambers, it was an extraordinary achievement for this ill-educated farm worker. In 1989, the whole construction was moved to La Fabuloserie, at Dicy, near Paris, by its founder Alain Bourbonnais; there it was painstakingly restored to its former glory.

Pierre Avezard (1909–1992), auch bekannt unter dem Pseudonym »Petit Pierre«, hatte eine Passion für Maschinen und komplexe mechanische Konstruktionen. Rund um sein abgelegenes Wohnhaus in Fay-aux-Loges bei Orléans schuf der Kuhhirte zwischen 1937 und 1974 ein lebhaftes Treiben von Zügen, Bussen, Flugzeugen und Straßenbahnen nebst Passagieren und Tieren, die auf Schienen und an diversen Drähten ihre Bahnen zogen. Das »Karussell« wurde nur durch ein einfaches Stellwerk gesteuert und war eine außergewöhnliche Leistung für den Landarbeiter ohne Ausbildung. 1989 wurde die gesamte Anlage von Alain Bourbonnais, dem Gründer von La Fabuloserie, nach Dicy bei Paris verlegt und sorgfältig restauriert.

Pierre Avezard (1909–1992), dit «Petit Pierre», gardait les vaches en rêvant de mécanique et de constructions compliquées. Entre 1937 et 1974, il construisit près de sa maison isolée, à Fay-aux-Loges, à proximité d'Orléans, son Manège où se croisaient en tous sens des trains, des autobus, des avions et des tramways avec leurs passagers, sans compter des animaux. Monté sur des

rails et des câbles, muni d'aiguillages rudimentaires, ce merveilleux automate représentait un véritable exploit pour un garçon de ferme n'ayant reçu aucune formation. En 1989, le Manège a été transporté à La Fabuloserie de Dicy, près de Paris, par Alain Bourbonnais, créateur du site: soigneusement restauré, il a ainsi été rendu à son ancienne splendeur.

Photo: Caroline Bourbonnais

The Manège clatters and whirs as the mass of metal objects jolts into controlled but seemingly anarchic movement.

Das Karussell von Petit Pierre wirkt geradezu anarchisch mit seinen klappernden und kreisenden Metallelementen, deren Bewegungen aber sorgfältig berechnet sind.

Le Manège virevolte et cliquette dans un tourbillon apparemment anarchique mais en fait soigneusement calculé.

LeMu séeRob ertTatin

Cossé-le-Vivien, France

Robert Tatin (1902–1983) had a variety of jobs, including circus performer and coalman, before becoming a ceramic artist in the Fifties. With his wife Elisabeth he bought a dilapidated farmhouse near Le Mans. After restoring the house, Tatin set to work in 1962 on a unique mystical environment. Approached by the "Avenue of Giants", where his heroes are depicted, the entrance to the central courtyard is guarded by an open-mouthed dragon. Within the courtyard is a temple-like structure intended to integrate the religions of the world and constitute a personal homage to himself and his wife. Around a pool stand three tall structures: Notre-Dame-Tout-Le-Monde (Our Lady Everyone), the Door of the Sun, and the Door of the Moon. After his death, Elisabeth completed Tatin's work and created a museum and gallery to display his paintings.

Photo: Jean-Pierre Alliot

Bevor **Robert Tatin** (1902–1983) sich in den fünfziger Jahren für die Arbeit als Künstler entschied, war er in den verschiedensten Berufen, auch als Zirkusartist und als Kohlenhändler, tätig gewesen. Er kaufte zusammen mit seiner Frau Elisabeth ein heruntergekommenes Bauernhaus bei Le Mans, renovierte es und begann 1962 mit der Errichtung einer einzigartigen mystischen Anlage. Die »Straße der Riesen« mit Tatins Lieblingshelden führt durch ein riesiges Drachenmaul zum Haupthof, wo eine tempelartige Anlage die Weltreligionen darstellt und gleichzeitig Tatin und seiner Frau huldigt. Drei große Bauwerke, Notre-Dame-Tout-Le-Monde, das Sonnen- und das Mondtor, säumen ein Wasserbecken. Nach Tatins Tod setzte Elisabeth die Arbeit fort und errichtete ein Museum und eine Galerie.

Robert Tatin (1902–1983) fit plusieurs métiers, bateleur et charbonnier entre autres, avant de devenir céramiste dans les années cinquante. Avec sa femme Elisabeth, il acheta et restaura une maison de campagne en ruine, près du Mans, puis il se lança en 1962 dans la création d'un étonnant site, empreint de mysticisme. L'«Allée des Géants», où se dressent ses grands héros, mène à l'entrée de la cour principale, gardée par un dragon à la gueule béante. A l'intérieur, Tatin a construit une sorte de temple, à la fois symbole des religions du monde entier et monument dédié au couple qu'il formait avec sa femme. L'ensemble se compose de trois hauts édifices: Notre-Dame-Tout-Le-Monde, la Porte du Soleil et la Porte de la Lune. Après la mort de son mari, Elisabeth a poursuivi son œuvre et créé un musée pour ses peintures.

The sculptures in which the inner courtyard abounds form part of its structure. They evoke the personal mythology of the artist.

Der Innnenhof ist reich geschmückt mit Figuren aus der persönlichen Mythologie des Künstlers, die sich harmonisch in die Architektur einfügen.

La cour intérieure regorge de sculptures faisant partie intégrante de l'architecture. Elles évoquent la mythologie personnelle de l'artiste, imprégnée de mysticisme.

DOUANIER ROUSSEAU

JEANNE—D'ARC

GAUGUIN

PABLO PICASSO

VERBE ÊTRE

SUZANNE VALADON ET UTRILLO

TOULOUSE LAUT

The "Avenue of Giants", which leads to the main temple compound, represents Robert Tatin's heroes in art, literature and history. The gaping mouth of a dragon guards the entrance (following pages).

An der »Straße der Riesen«, die zum Haupttempel führt, hat Tatin seine persönlichen Vorbilder aus Kunst, Literatur und Geschichte aufgestellt. Das furchterregende Drachenmaul bewacht den Eingang der Anlage (folgende Doppelseite).

L'«Allée des Géants», bordée par de grandes figures de l'art, de la littérature ou de l'histoire qu'admirait Tatin, mène à la cour principale. Un dragon à la gueule béante garde l'entrée (double page suivante).

LePal aisid éal

Hauterives, France

The Palais idéal (1879–1912), built by **Ferdinand Cheval** (1836–1924) near Lyon, is one of the world's most astounding visionary structures. The country postman was fascinated by unusually shaped stones and used them as raw material in his monumental quest to build the palace of his dreams. The product of 33 years of unaided toil, the Palais mixes Western and Oriental styles, and includes sculptural figures, beasts, twisting vine roots and concrete palm trees. Winding steps lead to turrets and columns encrusted with ornament. Beneath, a grotto-like crypt holds a shrine to the trusty wheelbarrow that was his daily companion in his search for materials. Along the east facade stand huge classical figures: Caesar, Vercingétorix and Archimedes. Tablets exhibit Cheval's poems and messages. At the age of 80, he was refused permission to use the Palais as his burying place, and so built for himself an extraordinary tomb in the local churchyard.

Der Palais idéal (1879–1912) des Land-briefträgers **Ferdinand Cheval** (1836–1924) in der Nähe von Lyon gehört zu den bemerkenswertesten phantastischen Bau-werken. Cheval war fasziniert von ungewöhnlich geformten Steinen und verwen-dete sie als Rohmaterial für seinen Traumpalast. Als Ergebnis 33jähriger harter Arbeit entstand eine Synthese östlicher und westlicher Architektur, geschmückt mit Figuren, Tieren und Palmen aus Beton. Gewundene Treppen führen hinauf zu reichverzierten Türmen und Säulen, während sich in der Krypta ein Schrein für Chevals Schubkarre befindet. An der Ostfassade ragen die Statuen von Cäsar, Vercingetorix und Archimedes empor. Auf Gedenktafeln hat Cheval Gedichte und Bot-schaften festgehalten. Als ihm die Erlaubnis für die Bestattung im Palais verweigert wurde, baute er mit 80 Jahren sein Grab auf dem Friedhof von Hauterives.

Le Palais idéal (1879–1912) construit par **Ferdinand Cheval** (1836–1924), facteur rural à Hauterives, près de Lyon, constitue l'un des sites inspirés les plus extraordinaires au monde. Pendant 33 ans, Cheval travailla en solitaire à l'achèvement de sa vision monumentale. Il était fasciné par les pierres de forme étrange, dont il fit le premier matériau pour bâtir le palais de ses rêves. Ici se mêlent architectures d'Orient et d'Occident, personnages gigantesques, animaux, palmiers en béton. Des escaliers courbes mènent à des tourelles et des colonnes. Au sous-sol, une crypte abrite la châsse de la fidèle brouette. Le long de la façade orientale se dressent les figures immenses de César, Vercingétorix et Archimède. Poèmes et inscriptions du facteur Cheval ornent les murs. Celui-ci avait 80 ans lorsqu'on lui refusa l'autorisation d'être enterré dans son Palais. Il édifia alors son tombeau dans le cimetière local.

Cheval's tomb in Hauterives cemetery, built in the last few years of his life (left). A crypt lies beneath the main arcaded structure, while stairways lead up to towers and walkways. Admired by the Surrealists, the Palais idéal was the very first visionary environment to be identified and documented as such.

Ferdinand Cheval errichtete in seinen letzten Lebensjahren auf dem Friedhof von Hauterives seine eigene Grabstätte (links). Unter den Arkaden des Hauptgebäudes befindet sich eine Krypta, diverse Treppen führen hinauf zu Türmen und Gängen. Der Palais idéal wurde von den Surrealisten sehr bewundert und als erstes Werk der phantastischen Architektur dokumentiert.

Cheval bâtit à la fin de sa vie son propre tombeau dans le cimetière de Hauterives (à gauche). L'édifice principal à arcades abrite une crypte, tandis qu'un escalier mène aux tours et aux galeries. Admiré par les surréalistes, le Palais idéal fut le tout premier site visionnaire reconnu et répertorié.

Le Parc-expo sitionRay mond Morales

Port de Bouc, France

In 1982 former blacksmith **Raymond Morales** (*1926) created his own museum exhibiting towering, frightening sculptures made of welded metal. Their bulbous eyes and anguished faces loom over the visitor, the cumulative effect enhanced by their rusting metallic textures. Morales' domain of 5000 square metres lies along the Mediterranean coast, near Marseilles, and is surrounded by a high wall topped by threatening metal faces. Within it stand more than 700 menacing figures, many of them a hybrid of human, animal and insect forms. New works are continually added. Morales is an outsider even in the outsider art world, but the uniquely powerful expression of his anguish has won him many admirers.

Raymond Morales (*1926), ein ehemaliger Schmied, schweißt aus Metall überdimensionale Skulpturen mit verzerrten Gesichtern, die aus hervorquellenden Augen auf den Besucher herabblicken. Seit 1982 stellt er sie in seinem eigenen Museum aus, dessen Sammlung er ständig erweitert. Im Lauf der Jahre haben die mehr als 700 Skulpturen, die hybride Formen von Mensch, Tier und Insekt aufweisen, Rost angesetzt, was ihr finsteres Aussehen noch verstärkt. Eine hohe Mauer mit bedrohlichen Fratzen aus Metall umgibt das Gelände in der Nähe von Marseille, das 5000 Quadratmeter umfaßt. Der Kunstwelt und selbst derjenigen der Outsider Artists verweigerte Morales sich stets, und trotzdem hat sein Werk mit der einzigartigen Ausstrahlung von Angst und Schmerz viele Bewunderer gefunden.

The huge and menacing iron figures, many a combination of grotesque human and insect forms, parade around Raymond Morales' walled compound.

In der ummauerten Anlage von Raymond Morales sind bedrohliche Eisenskulpturen aufgestellt, die Insektenformen mit menschlichen Zügen mischen.

Derrière de hauts murs se dresse une foule métallique de grandes sculptures menaçantes, animaux, insectes ou personnages grotesques.

Ancien forgeron, **Raymond Morales** (*1926) créa en 1982 son propre parc de sculptures en métal soudé, peuplé de grands personnages inquiétants à l'expression angoissée. Leurs yeux globuleux plongent sur le visiteur, dans une atmosphère que la rouille rend plus sombre encore. A l'abri d'un haut mur couronné de têtes en métal menaçantes, exposées sur un terrain de plus de 5000 mètres carrés, plus de 700 créatures, pour la plupart des hybrides d'homme, d'animaux et d'insectes, se dressent sur la côte, non loin de Marseille. Continuant à travailler sur la collection, Morales préfère se tenir à l'écart du milieu de l'art, fût-il brut, mais ses œuvres, si particulières par l'angoisse qu'elles dégagent, ont toutefois séduit de nombreux admirateurs.

Il Parco dei tarocchi

Garavicchio, Italy

The work of **Niki de Saint Phalle** (1930–2002) is well known in the field of 20th century art. Influenced by figures such as Jean Dubuffet and Antoni Gaudí, she made her reputation in the Sixties with a series of giant female figures, the "Nanas". Visitors could walk inside "Hon", which was installed at the Moderna Museet in Stockholm in 1966. She collaborated with sculptor Jean Tinguely on large scale sculptural projects, and since 1979 had been working on the enormous Tarot Garden in Tuscany. Financed by the sale of her art around the world and built with the help of local artists and craftsmen, the structures have strong steel frames designed by Jean Tinguely and are overlaid with sprayed concrete, then covered in shimmering mirror and ceramic mosaics. The High Priestess represents the feminine principal of the universe. The huge blue-lipped mouth is a fountain whence water cascades down the steps to a pond. The elaborate interior of the Magician has been richly painted by Scottish artist Alan Davie. Inspired by the 22 Major Arcana of the Tarot, these colossal architectural sculptures serve as a lasting monument to Saint Phalle's creative energies.

Niki de Saint Phalle (1930–2002) gehörte zu den wichtigen Künstlern des 20. Jahrhunderts. Bekannt wurde sie in den sechziger Jahren mit ihren »Nanas«, monumentalen Frauenfiguren wie die begehbare Skulptur »Hon«, die 1966 im Stockholmer Moderna Museet ausgestellt wurde. Beeinflußt wurde Saint Phalle von Jean Dubuffet und Antoni Gaudí. Sie realisierte gemeinsam mit dem Bildhauer Jean Tinguely mehrere größere Projekte und begann 1979 die Gestaltung des riesigen Tarotgartens in der Toskana. Den Bau finanzierte sie mit dem Verkauf ihrer Kunstwerke, während sie bei der Ausführung von toskanischen Künstlern und Handwerkern unterstützt wurde. Die gewaltigen Skulpturen bestehen im Kern aus starken, von Tinguely konstruierten Stahlgerüsten, die mit Zement bedeckt und anschließend mit schimmernden Spiegel- und Keramikmosaiken verziert werden. Vorbild der Figuren sind die 22 Großen Arkana des Tarot. Der Magier wurde von dem schottischen Künstler Alan Davie innen reich bemalt. Eine weitere Skulptur ist die Hohepriesterin, die das weibliche Prinzip des Universums darstellt. Aus ihren gewaltigen blauen Lippen ergießt sich Wasser über Treppenstufen kaskadenartig in einen Teich. Die überdimensionalen Skulpturen bezeugen das reiche kreative Potential von Niki de Saint Phalle.

Photo: Roger Guillemot/Bernard Saint-Genès

Niki de Saint Phalle (1930–2002) fut une figure célèbre de l'art au XXe siècle. Influencée par des artistes comme Jean Dubuffet et Antoni Gaudí, elle s'était fait connaître dans les années soixante avec ses personnages féminins géants, les «Nanas», dont certains se visitent de l'intérieur, comme la «Hon», exposée en 1966 au Moderna Museet de Stockholm. Niki de Saint Phalle avait créé en collaboration avec Jean Tinguely des sculptures de grandes dimensions. Depuis 1979, elle travailla en Toscane à la réalisation de l'énorme Parc des Tarots, avec l'aide d'artistes et d'artisans locaux; le projet fut financé par la vente de ses œuvres. Les différents éléments du parc sont composés de structures très résistantes en acier, conçues par Jean Tinguely, recouvertes de béton et entièrement décorées de mosaïques en céramique et en miroir. Représentant le principe féminin de l'univers, la Papesse crache de l'eau par son énorme bouche bleue, cascade qui aboutit à un bassin après avoir dévalé un escalier. L'artiste écossais Alan Davie a peint de façon somptueuse l'intérieur très élaboré du Bateleur. Inspirées des 22 arcanes majeurs du tarot, ces colossales sculptures architecturales témoignent de l'inventivité exubérante de Niki de Saint Phalle.

The High Priestess (card II), flanked by the Tower (card XVI), gazes out across the Tuscany hillside (left). The Empress (card III) served as Saint Phalle's house and studio (above).

Die Hohepriesterin (Karte II) und der Turm (Karte XVI) überragen das toskanische Hügelland (links). In der Herrscherin (Karte III) befanden sich Wohnung und Atelier von Niki de Saint Phalle (oben).

La Papesse (arcane II), flanquée de la Maison-Dieu (carte XVI), scrute les collines toscanes (à gauche). L'Impératrice (carte III) abritait l'habitation et l'atelier de Niki de Saint Phalle (ci-dessus).

Facing page: the Hierophant (card V); above left: Justice (card VIII); above right: the Serpent Tree, symbolising the Tree of Life; left: inscriptions carved into the wet cement of a path; right: the Hanged Man (card XII) on a background of sparkling mirrored mosaic.

Linke Seite: Der Papst (Karte V); oben links: die Gerechtigkeit (Karte VIII); oben rechts: der Schlangenbaum symbolisiert den Lebensbaum; links: auf dem feuchten Zement hat die Künstlerin Inschriften eingeritzt; rechts: der Gehängte (Karte XII) befindet sich vor einer Wand mit glitzernden Spiegelmosaiken.

Page de gauche: le Pape (carte V); ci-dessus à gauche: la Justice (carte VIII); ci-dessus à droite: l'Arbre-Serpent symbolisant l'Arbre de Vie; à gauche: inscriptions gravées dans le ciment d'un sentier; à droite: le Pendu (carte XII), devant un mur étincelant de mosaïques en miroir.

LesRoc herssc ulptés

Rothéneuf, France

A hermit priest, the **Abbé Adolphe Julien Fouré** (1839–1910), with the aid of an elderly helper, spent 25 years carving the granite rocks of the Brittany shoreline at Rothéneuf. Abbé Fouré was partly paralysed by a stroke and had lost his hearing and speech. In his isolation, he was inspired by old tales of a local pirate clan. The carvings, numbering over 300 pieces in an area of 600 square metres, depict legendary pirate adventurers, fisherman, smugglers, sea monsters and allegorical scenes. Begun in 1870, the Carved Rocks have a timeless quality; although many were carved from free standing rocks, others follow the natural contours of the shore. Fouré was also a prolific wood carver, but his underground gallery of wooden sculptures was destroyed by fire during the Allied advance in 1944, and only a few works have survived.

In 25jähriger Arbeit meißelten der Priester **Abbé Adolphe Julien Fouré** (1839–1910) und ein betagter Helfer Reliefs in die Granitfelsen der bretonischen Küste. Fouré war seit einem Schlaganfall taubstumm und lebte sehr zurückgezogen. Er ließ sich inspirieren von alten Sagen über einen lokalen Piratenclan und gestaltete auf einer Fläche von ungefähr 600 Quadratmetern mehr als 300 Skulpturen, darunter Fischer, Schmuggler, Meeresungeheuer sowie allegorische Darstellungen. Sein 1870 begonnenes Werk ist zeitlos und umfaßt bearbeitete freistehende Felsen wie auch Szenen, die er aus dem natürlichen Verlauf der Steilküste herausmeißelte. Der Künstler war auch ein begabter Holzschnitzer, doch seine unterirdische Galerie wurde während der Invasion der Alliierten 1944 durch ein Feuer fast völlig zerstört.

L'abbé **Adolphe Julien Fouré** (1839–1910) consacra 25 ans de sa vie à sculpter les rochers granitiques de la côte bretonne, à Rothéneuf. Hémiplégique, ayant perdu l'ouïe et la parole, il vivait en ermite et travaillait avec la seule aide d'un vieil homme. S'inspirant des légendes liées à une famille de corsaires de la région, il créa plus de 300 sculptures sur une superficie de 600 mètres carrés. Les sculptures représentent des pirates, des pêcheurs, des contrebandiers, des monstres marins et des scènes allégoriques. Commencées en 1870, elles ont un caractère intemporel. Bon nombre de figures sont taillées dans des rochers isolés mais d'autres suivent les contours naturels de la côte. L'abbé Fouré réalisa aussi de nombreuses pièces en bois. Entreposées dans une galerie souterraine, elles disparurent dans un incendie lors du débarquement allié, en 1944; seules quelques-unes sont parvenues jusqu'à nous.

The imposing granite faces gaze out across the sea, while the bedrock is carved as if by nature's hand.

Eindrucksvolle Granitköpfe blicken auf das Meer, unter ihnen die alterslosen Skulpturen.

Les imposantes têtes en granit scrutent l'horizon, tandis qu'au sol grouillent des sculptures sans âge.

La Scar zuola

Montegabbione, Italy

Architect **Tomaso Buzzi** (1900–1981) began work on his La Scarzuola complex, near Orvieto, in 1958, intending to create a Utopian centre for the arts around an abandoned convent. At the centre of the complex is the Acropolis, on which stand pastiches of classical architecture, including scaled-down versions of the Pantheon, Parthenon, and Colosseum. There are seven "theatres", where different events or productions can take place simultaneously, and a huge open air auditorium. Within a conical glass pyramid topped by a golden star rises a seven octave staircase, each tread giving out a different note. Buzzi worked on his grand project until 1978. Abandoned and overgrown after his death, La Scarzuola is now awaiting visitors. It has been restored under the direction of Buzzi's grand-nephew, Marco Solari, using original sketches and plans.

1958 entwarf der Architekt **Tomaso Buzzi** (1900–1981) La Scarzuola als ein utopisches Zentrum für Kunst in einem verlassenen Kloster bei Orvieto. Das Herz des Komplexes bildet die Akropolis, die verschiedene Beispiele klassischer Architektur in sich vereint, u.a. Miniaturmodelle des römischen Pantheons, des Kolosseums und des Parthenons. Zu La Scarzuola gehören ein riesiges Freiluftauditorium sowie sieben Theater, in denen verschiedene Stücke gleichzeitig aufgeführt werden können. In einer Glaspyramide mit goldenem Stern auf der Spitze installierte Buzzi eine klingende Treppe: Beim Betreten der einzelnen Stufen sind jeweils andere Töne zu hören, die insgesamt sieben Oktaven umfassen. Buzzi arbeitete bis 1978 an der Anlage, doch nach seinem Tod geriet sie in Vergessenheit und verfiel. Heute wird sie von Buzzis Großneffen Marco Solari nach den Originalplänen restauriert, und sie ist inzwischen wieder zugänglich.

L'architecte **Tomaso Buzzi** (1900–1981) a commencé en 1958 à travailler à son grand projet d'un centre utopiste des arts sur le site d'un ancien couvent, non loin d'Orvieto. Au cœur du complexe se trouve l'Acropole, un pastiche de différents monuments antiques où se mêlent des versions réduites du Panthéon de Rome, du Colisée et du Parthénon. On trouve à La Scarzuola sept salles de spectacle où des manifestations différentes peuvent avoir lieu simultanément, ainsi qu'un immense auditorium à ciel ouvert. Une pyramide conique surmontée d'une étoile dorée abrite un escalier musical à sept octaves, où chaque marche produit une note différente. Buzzi a poursuivi son travail jusqu'à 1978. Après sa mort les lieux ont été abandonnés et envahis par la végétation. Marco Solari, petit-neveu de l'architecte, en a désormais entrepris la restauration, en utilisant les croquis et les plans d'origine. Ont peut aujourd'hui à nouveau visiter La Scarzuola.

The open mouth of Jonah's Whale leads to a forest of columns, the Gate of Bees and the circular Wall of Memory with its dead cypress tree (right). Celestial symbols adorning the structure include a golden comet surmounting the crystal pyramid.

Durch das Maul von Jonas' Wal gelangt man in einen Säulenwald, zum Bienentor und zu der kreisrunden Erinnerungsmauer, die von einer toten Zypresse überragt wird (rechts). Himmelssymbole, darunter ein goldener Komet auf einer Kristallpyramide, zieren die Anlage.

Par la gueule béante de la baleine de Jonas, on accède à une forêt de colonnes, à la Porte des Abeilles et au Mur du Souvenir, enceinte circulaire qui abrite un cyprès mort (à droite). Des symboles célestes ornent l'ensemble, parmi lesquels une comète dorée surmontant la pyramide de cristal.

The Tower of Meditation (top left) and views of the Amphitheatre (top right), the Grand Theatre and the Theatre of Bees (above). The Water Theatre leads up to the Step Pyramid of the Nymph Echo (right and facing page).

Zur Anlage gehören der Meditationsturm (ganz oben links), das Amphitheater (ganz oben rechts), das Große Theater und das Bienentheater (oben). Das Wassertheater führt hinauf zur Stufenpyramide der Nymphe Echo (rechts und rechte Seite).

La Tour de Méditation (tout en haut à gauche), l'Amphithéâtre (tout en haut à droite), le Grand Théâtre et le Théâtre des Abeilles (ci-dessus). Le Théâtre de l'Eau mène à la pyramide à degrés de la Nymphe Echo (à droite et page de droite).

TheSed lecOs suary

Sedlec, Czech Republic

The Sedlec cemetery near Kutná Hora was founded in the late 13th century by a Cistercian abbot. The burial ground proved popular with monks and the devout; by the end of the 15th century, 40 000 people had been buried there. Skeletons were stacked in the charnel house and catacombs, which gradually filled to overflowing. In the late 19th century, sculptor **František Rint** was commissioned to create a sculptural decoration using the countless bones in the ossuary. The centrepiece is the Schwarzenberg coat of arms, painstakingly recreated in bone and surrounded by strings of skulls and decorative arrangements.

Der Friedhof von Sedlec bei Kutná Hora wurde Ende des 13. Jahrhunderts von einem Zisterzienserabt gegründet und war als letzte Ruhestätte bei Mönchen und Gläubigen sehr beliebt. Bis zum Ende des 15. Jahrhunderts hatten dort ungefähr 40 000 Begräbnisse stattgefunden. Die zahllosen Skelette wurden im Beinhaus und in den Katakomben aufbewahrt. Ende des 19. Jahrhunderts wurde der Bildhauer **František Rint** damit beauftragt, die Knochen im Beinhaus in ornamentalen Formen zu arrangieren. Sein Hauptwerk bildet das aus Knochen sorgfältig nachgebildete und von einer Schädelgirlande gerahmte Schwarzenberg-Wappen.

Créé à la fin du 13e siècle par un abbé cistercien, le cimetière de Sedlec près de Kutná Hora abritait à la fin du 15e siècle les dépouilles de 40 000 moines et chrétiens. Devant cet afflux, quantité de squelettes furent remisés dans un bâtiment et dans des catacombes, qui s'avérèrent à leur tour trop exigus. A la fin du 19e siècle, le sculpteur **František Rint** fut chargé d'aménager avec art ces innombrables ossements, dans l'enceinte même du cimetière. Les armes des Schwarzenberg constituent l'élément central de la composition: le motif, soigneusement reproduit avec des os, est encadré d'une guirlande de crânes et d'ornementations.

The interior of the Ossuary is hung with garlands of skulls which set off the magnificent Schwarzenberg coat of arms (facing page). Above: a chalice of bones and Rint's own memorial.

Schädelketten, ein Kelch aus Knochen sowie eine Gedenkinschrift für Rint sind im Inneren des Beinhauses zu sehen. Das eindrucksvolle Schwarzenberg-Wappen (rechte Seite) ist aus Schädeln arrangiert.

L'intérieur de l'ossuaire s'orne de guirlandes de crânes, d'un calice en os et d'une plaque avec le nom du sculpteur. Page de droite: les armes des Schwarzenberg, encadrées de crânes.

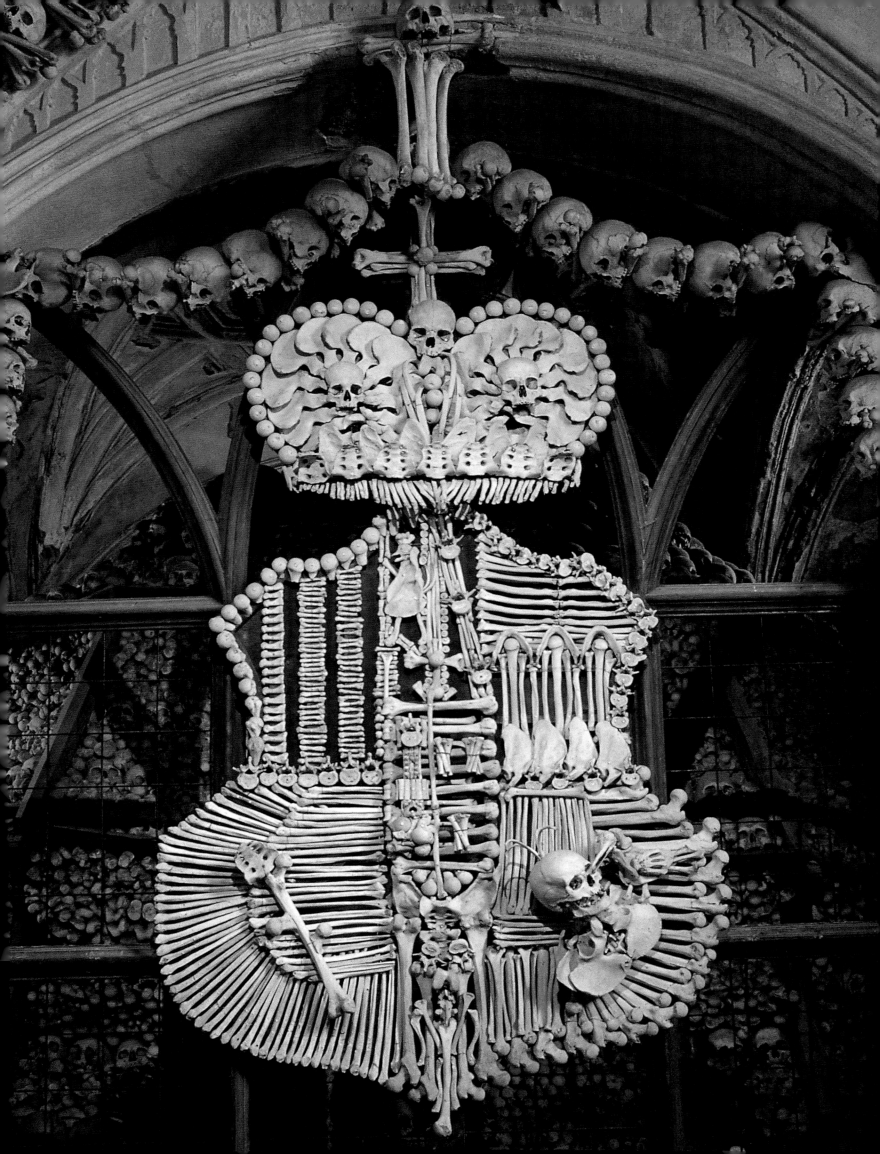

La Tour de l'Apocalypse

Eben-Emael, Belgium

Inspired by the Book of Revelations, **Robert Garcet** (1912–2001), a former quarryman, built his seven-storey, 20-metre tower (1948–1963) as a monument to peace. Constructed with the help of family and friends, its external walls are faced with flint. Huge winged sculptures representing the four Evangelists stand menacingly at the corners of the summit. Beneath the tower lie 800 metres of disused flint-mining tunnels, which have become Garcet's underground museum, a repository for his artefacts and paintings. Garcet has evolved his own theory of history, believing that a civilisation existed 70 million years ago and that flints are its sculptures.

Das neutestamentarische Buch der Offenbarung inspirierte **Robert Garcet** (1912–2001), einen ehemaligen Steinbrucharbeiter, zum Bau eines 20 Meter hohen Turmes (1948–1963) mit sieben Stockwerken. Gemeinsam mit Familienangehörigen und Freunden errichtete er dieses Mahnmal des Friedens bei Lüttich und verkleidete es außen mit Feuerstein. Auf den vier Ecken des Turmes stehen drohend monumentale geflügelte Tiere, die die Evangelisten symbolisieren. Weitere Artefakte und Gemälde sind in den 800 Meter langen Gängen einer ehemaligen Feuersteinmine ausgestellt, die Garcet zu einem unterirdischen Museum umgestaltet hat. Der Künstler hat eine eigene Theorie der Menschheitsgeschichte entwickelt, nach der Feuersteine die Relikte einer vor 70 Millionen Jahren untergegangenen Kultur sind.

Inspiré par l'Apocalypse, **Robert Garcet** (1912–2001) a conçu près de Liège sa tour de sept étages, haute de 20 mètres, comme un monument à la paix (1948–1963). Cet ancien ouvrier carrier a travaillé avec l'aide de sa famille et d'amis. Les murs extérieurs de la tour sont incrustés de silex. D'immenses créatures ailées représentent les quatre évangélistes surmontent, menaçantes, les angles du bâtiment. En sous-sol, 800 mètres de galeries désaffectées, d'où l'on extrayait autrefois le silex, abritent un musée souterrain qui regroupe les objets et les peintures créés par Robert Garcet. Ce dernier a élaboré sa propre théorie de l'histoire, selon laquelle la civilisation existait déjà voici 70 millions d'années: les silex seraient des sculptures de ces temps lointains.

The vast threatening figures of the four Beasts of the Apocalypse gaze down from the top of the Tower.

Drohend blicken die vier geflügelten Tiere der Apokalypse vom Turm herab.

Menaçantes, les quatre Bêtes de l'Apocalypse nous observent du haut des tours.

A sculpture of a dinosaur (left) guards the entrance to the underground museum beneath the Tower, where Garcet displays his collection of prehistoric artifacts alongside his sculptures and paintings.

Ein Dinosaurier (links) bewacht den Eingang zu dem unterirdischen Museum, in dem Robert Garcet seine Sammlung prähistorischer Artefakte neben seinen Skulpturen und Gemälden ausstellt.

Un dinosaure (à gauche) surveille l'entrée du musée souterrain dans lequel Robert Garcet expose sa collection d'objets préhistoriques à côté de ses sculptures et de ses tableaux.

On the main floor of the tower, a column repeats the motif of the four Beasts of the Apocalypse (facing page).

An einer Säule auf der Hauptetage des Turmes wiederholt sich das Motiv der vier Tiere der Apokalypse (rechte Seite).

Le motif des Bêtes de l'Apocalypse se répète sur une colonne de l'étage principal de la tour (page de droite).

The Josef Váchal Mus eum

Litomyšl, Czech Republic

The art lover and retired clerk Josef Portman, a great admirer of the artist **Josef Váchal** (1884–1969), commissioned him to cover the inner walls of his house near Prague with murals. Portman planned to open the building as a museum dedicated to Váchal's work, but was unable to arrange this. In 1991, the Prague publishing house Paseka purchased the house and extensively restored the interior, saving Váchal's paintings. 70 years after the museum was first planned, it finally opened its doors. Váchal began his work in 1920, painting a ceiling and a wardrobe. The following year, he created further decorations in carved wood and paint. In 1924 he returned, and in a ten-day creative burst painted almost all the rest of the house. Portman was unable to persuade Váchal to return and embellish his work with carvings; the artist was by now involved in writing "Blood Novel", which was published by Paseka in 1990.

Photo: Zdeněk Helfert

Der pensionierte Angestellte, Kunstliebhaber und Drucker Josef Portman schätzte den Künstler **Josef Váchal** (1884–1969) sehr und beauftragte ihn damit, sein Haus bei Prag auszumalen. Ursprünglich wollte er das Gebäude als Váchal-Museum eröffnen, setzte diesen Plan jedoch nie in die Tat um. 1991 wurde der Bau von dem Prager Verlagshaus Paseka aufgekauft, mitsamt Váchals Werken aufwendig renoviert und 70 Jahre später als geplant doch noch als Museum eröffnet. 1920 hatte Váchal nur die Garderobe und eine Zimmerdecke gestaltet und ein Jahr später einige Dekorationen und Holzschnitzereien angebracht. 1924 bemalte er dann in einem wahren Ausbruch an Kreativität innerhalb von zehn Tagen den Rest des Hauses. Portman konnte den Künstler allerdings nicht dazu bewegen, weitere Holzschnitzereien anzubringen, denn Váchal zog es vor, an seinem Roman »Blood Novel« zu arbeiten, der von Paseka 1990 veröffentlicht wurde.

Grand admirateur de **Josef Váchal** (1884–1969), Josef Portman, amateur d'art et ancien employé, demanda à l'artiste de décorer de peintures murales l'intérieur de sa maison, près de Prague. Portman prévoyait de faire de sa demeure un musée consacré au peintre: hélas, le projet ne vit jamais le jour. Il s'est concrétisé 70 ans plus tard, en 1991, lorsque les éditions pragoises Paseka ont racheté et restauré les lieux, sauvant ainsi les œuvres de Váchal. En 1920, ce dernier avait commencé par peindre un plafond et une penderie puis, l'année suivante, il avait réalisé d'autres décorations peintes ou en bois. Enfin, en 1924, saisi d'inspiration, il peignit pratiquement tout le reste de la demeure en une dizaine de jours. Il n'y retravailla jamais, malgré les instances de Portman qui souhaitait le voir créer d'autres ornements sculptés. Váchal préféra se consacrer à la rédaction de son roman, «Blood Novel», publié par Paseka en 1990.

The intense imagery of Váchal's murals is dominated by Christian iconography, occult symbology and quotations from the ancient Hindu epic, the "Bhagavad Gita".

Die kraftvolle Bildsprache von Josef Váchal verbindet christliche Ikonographie mit okkulter Symbolik und Zitaten aus dem alten indischen Epos »Bhagavad Gita«.

Le puissant vocabulaire pictural de Josef Váchal marie l'iconographie chrétienne, la symbolique de l'occultisme et des citations de la «Bhagavad Gita», le grand poème épique de l'Inde ancienne.

Le Village d'Art preludien

Chomo (Roger Chomeaux, 1907–1999) trained as an artist, but after receiving no response from his first exhibition, in the Sixties, he retired to a reclusive existence on a plot of land near Fontainebleau, busying himself with his Village of Preludian Art. A collection of buildings constructed from reclaimed materials is surrounded by thousands of sculptures and assemblages. Some of the buildings house collections of his paintings. His varying styles have included figures made of entwined and painted chicken wire and others of carved building blocks or scorched wood. The woods around his compound are adorned with small sculptures, while Chomo's many phonetically-spelled mottos and exhortations hang from the branches.

Chomo (Roger Chomeaux, 1907–1999), ein ausgebildeter Künstler, zog sich nach dem Mißerfolg seiner ersten Ausstellung in den sechziger Jahren auf seinen Besitz bei Fontainebleau zurück, wo er sich ausschließlich seinem »Dorf« widmete. Er errichtete aus Trödel verschiedene Bauwerke, die er mit Tausenden von Skulpturen und Assemblagen umgab. Die enorme Bandbreite seiner Werke umfaßt Figuren aus verschlungenem und bemaltem Draht, gemeißeltem Stein oder versengtem Holz. In einigen Gebäuden sind seine zahllosen Gemälde ausgestellt. Im angrenzenden Wald stehen kleine Skulpturen, und an den Zweigen hängen Chomos Kalligraphien.

Après une formation artistique, **Chomo** (Roger Chomeaux, 1907–1999) réalise sa première exposition dans les années soixante mais son œuvre ne rencontre pas d'écho. Il choisit alors de mener une existence solitaire consacrée à la création, dans sa propriété située près de Fontainebleau. Des milliers de sculptures et d'assemblages entourent des édifices construits à partir de matériaux de récupération; certains de ces bâtiments abritent les innombrables peintures de Chomo. L'artiste a adopté différents styles et techniques, réalisant entre autres des personnages en fil de fer peint, en parpaings sculptés ou en bois brûlé. Les futaies alentour sont ornées de petites sculptures tandis que de nombreuses pancartes suspendues aux branches portent les inscriptions phonétiques des devises et des exhortations de Chomo.

Visitors are greeted with signs in Chomo's own brand of calligraphy. Burnt wood is one of the many mediums Chomo has used for his sculptures. Chomo's buildings have walls of inlaid bottles and roofs of reclaimed car bodies.

Der Besucher wird begrüßt von Chomos Kalligraphien, die in Holz eingebrannt sind – nur eine der vielen Techniken, in denen der Künstler seine Werke ausführte. Autoteile bedecken die Gebäude, in deren Wände Flaschen eingelassen sind.

Le visiteur est accueilli par les calligraphies de Chomo, pyrogravées sur bois – une des nombreuses techniques utilisées par l'artiste. Les bâtiments de Chomo ont des toits faits de pièces de voitures et des murs incrustés de bouteilles.

Chomo's vast collection of sculptures stand all around the environment. Inside the buildings, the light streams through arrangements of coloured bottles inlaid into the walls.

Chomos umfangreiche Skulpturensammlung ist auf dem gesamten Gelände ausgestellt. Durch gefärbtes Flaschenglas strömt Licht in das Innere der Gebäude.

La vaste collection de sculptures de Chomo est répartie sur tout le terrain. La lumière traverse les bouteilles colorées insérées dans les murs et éclaire l'intérieur du bâtiment.

DerWeinr ebenpark

Dietikon, Switzerland

Bruno Weber (*1931) studied fine art and graphic design before inheriting his property at Dietikon near Zurich in 1962. There he and his wife Marianne Weber-Prot built and decorated a studio, which he gradually expanded. Under the influence of Greek mythology and Gothic and oriental architecture, they have created Vine Park, a monumental piece of sculptural architecture. Bruno Weber lacked funds, but was able to barter his paintings, sculptures and plastic moulded furniture for building materials. The large-scale sculptures in the garden include a cat-headed elephant, a cow and a bull with robotic heads, a woman-sunflower with a child, and a dragon that acts a a giant slide. Twenty oriental wise men double as seats on the winding paths that link the totem poles, the two 22-metre towers, facades of relief sculpture, columns, a water garden, and gates shaped like animals. His huge sculptures are constructed around strong architectural frames. The house serves as a family home, but resembles a fantastical palazzo, with brightly coloured ceramic fragments embedded in concrete columns and walls. Weber is a prolific creator: his plans for the future include a sun-shaped mirror for mass-production and a village of head-shaped houses to be constructed on an island.

1962 erbte **Bruno Weber** (*1931) ein Grundstück in Dietikon bei Zürich, auf dem er gemeinsam mit seiner Frau Marianne Weber-Prot ein Atelier errichtete. Zuvor hatte Weber an der Züricher Kunstgewerbeschule studiert und als Lithograph gearbeitet. Die Baumaterialien für seinen »Palazzo« erhielt er im Tausch gegen seine Gemälde, Skulpturen und selbstentworfenen Plastikmöbel. Die monumentale Bauskulptur orientiert sich an der griechischen Mythologie, gotischer sowie orientalischer Architektur und spiegelt Webers eigene phantastische Welt. Im Garten stehen riesige Statuen, darunter ein Elefant mit Katzenkopf, eine Kuh und ein Bulle mit Roboterköpfen, eine Kreuzung aus Frau und Sonnenblume mit Kind, ein überdimensionaler Schlitten in Form eines Drachens und 20 orientalische Weise, die als Sitzgelegenheiten dienen. Gewundene Pfade führen zu mehreren Totempfählen, zwei Türmen von 22 Metern Höhe, Fassaden mit Reliefschmuck, verschiedenen Säulen, einem Wassergarten und mehreren Toren in Tierformen. Die Wände und Säulen des Ateliers, in dem die Familie Weber auch wohnt, sind mit farbenprächtigen Keramikstücken bedeckt. Der Künstler steckt voller Pläne für neue Projekte, darunter die Serienproduktion eines sonnenförmigen Spiegels und der Bau eines Inseldorfes mit Häusern in Kopfform.

Après avoir étudié les beaux-arts à Zurich, **Bruno Weber** (*1931) devient designer. En 1962, il hérite d'une propriété à Dietikon, où il aménage, avec sa femme Marianne Weber-Prot, un atelier qu'il décore puis qu'il agrandit. Influencé par la mythologie grecque et par les architectures gothique et asiatique, Weber a donné corps à un univers visionnaire, le Parc des vignes, où se mêlent édifices et sculptures aux proportions impressionnantes. L'artiste se procure les matériaux nécessaires en échange de ses peintures, sculptures et meubles en plastique moulé. Parmi les grandes figures du jardin se dressent un éléphant à face de chat, une vache et un taureau à têtes d'automate, une femme-tournesol avec un enfant, un dragon qui fait office de toboggan géant et 20 sages orientaux servant de sièges. Des chemins sinueux relient des totems, deux tours hautes de 22 mètres, des édifices couverts de bas-reliefs, des

colonnes, un jardin d'eau et des portails aux formes animales. Les énormes sculptures sont soutenues par des éléments architectoniques. Sorte de palais fantastique où vit la famille de Weber, la maison est décorée de mosaïques colorées en céramique incrustées dans le ciment recouvrant les parois et les colonnes. Le maître des lieux, en travailleur acharné, a de nombreux projets parmi lesquels un miroir-soleil à fabriquer en série et un village de maisons en forme de têtes, à construire sur une île.

Bruno Weber's Vine Park, covering an area of five acres, is approached through a gateway (following pages).

Das Portal bildet den Eingang zum Weinrebenpark, der sich über zwei Hektar erstreckt (folgende Doppelseite).

Le portail mène au Parc des vignes, qui s'étend sur deux hectares (double page suivante).

America Amerika Amérique

The ArtYard

Centralia, Washington

"Looking Out for the Herd" was constructed in just five hours from reclaimed materials (below). Inside the street frontage Richart has built 55 animal constructions, among them one made of old gun racks (page 137).

»Das Hüten der Herde« wurde in nur fünf Stunden aus Fundmaterialien errichtet (unten). Vor der Fassade stehen 55 Tierskulpturen, darunter eine aus alten Gewehrständern (Seite 137).

Richart a construit en cinq heures seulement, à partir de matériaux récupérés, cet ensemble intitulé «En surveillant le bétail» (ci-dessous). Côté route, il a réalisé 55 constructions zoomorphes, dont certaines avec de vieux râteliers à fusils (page 137).

Using a mixture of wooden poles and styrofoam, **Richard Tracy** (*1933) has, since 1985, built a closely packed jungle of white-painted forms. Styrofoam, reclaimed packaging material, is carved into faces and archaic forms before being attached to tall poles. The whiteness of the environment imparts an eerie unity. Tracy is known as Richart, "Rich Art", and his environment has absorbed all manner of found objects: old shoes, washtubs, flower pots and brushes. Tracy has also made animals in crudely welded metal; some of these stand at the roadside frontage, while others lie deep inside the labyrinthine complex.

At its heart is his own hideaway, his "confessional", where he can sit and enjoy the view over the outside world. Tracy is well-educated and gives lessons to art students, encouraging them to follow his own unique methods of working.

Richard Tracy (*1933) gestaltete aus Styropor und Verpackungsmaterial Gesichter und archaische Formen, die er weiß bemalte und auf langen Pfählen befestigte. So entstand ab 1985 ein regelrechter Dschungel aus unheimlich wirkenden Skulpturen. Tracy ist bekannt unter dem Pseudonym Richart (Rich in Art, »der Kunstvolle«). Für seine phantastische Welt verwendete er Fundstücke jeglicher Art, wie Schuhe, Wannen, Blumentöpfe und Pinsel. Aus Metall zusammengeschweißte Tierfiguren stehen direkt an der Straße, aber auch tief in der labyrinthartigen Anlage versteckt, wo sich auch ein geheimer Schlupfwinkel befindet, der »Beichtstuhl«. Hierhin zieht sich Tracy zurück, wenn er nicht gerade Kunststudenten dazu ermuntert, ihre eigenen Arbeitsweisen zu entwickeln.

Richard Tracy (*1933) a créé, à l'aide de poteaux de bois et de polystyrène, une véritable forêt de silhouettes blanches. Il sculpte à partir de 1985 des visages et des formes primitives dans du polystyrène récupéré dans des emballages, et les fixe sur de longs pieux. Tout est peint en blanc: une atmosphère étrange, fantomatique, règne sur l'endroit. Surnommé Richart (Rich Art ou «art riche»), il emploie toutes sortes d'objets de récupération: vieilles chaussures, cuvettes, pots de fleurs, brosses, etc. Il fabrique aussi des animaux en métal sommairement soudé, dont certains se dressent au bord de la route tandis que d'autres nichent dans le secret de sa jungle. C'est là que Tracy a sa propre cachette, qu'il appelle «le confessionnal», et d'où il peut observer en paix le monde extérieur. Possédant une formation de bon niveau, il accepte toujours des élèves, qu'il encourage à suivre ses méthodes de travail originales.

The Bottle Castle

Duncan, British Columbia, Canada

George Plumb († 1976) bought a site measuring just over an acre in 1962; a year later, he set to work with 5 000 bottles. A former carpenter, he built his little five-roomed house out of every conceivable type of bottle, collected from local industries and donated by neighbours and visitors. Over the years, he used a total of 200 000 bottles. The structures around the main building included a Leaning Tower of Pisa, a Taj Mahal, a well, and a giant bottle of Coke, all constructed of bottles and cement. Plumb surrounded his buildings with animals, some of them sculpted in concrete, others carved in stone. In the gardens, paths between low walls led past flower beds to a small waterfall, water-lily and fish ponds, a totem pole and a small studio. After his death the complex was run as a low-grade tourist attraction, but it has since fallen into disrepair.

1962 erwarb **George Plumb** († 1976) einen halben Hektar Land und begann ein Jahr später, aus 5 000 Flaschen ein Häuschen mit fünf Zimmern zu errichten. Die Flaschen hatte der ehemalige Schreiner bei den umliegenden Fabriken gesammelt oder von Nachbarn und Besuchern geschenkt bekommen. Insgesamt verbaute er im Lauf der Jahre mehr als 200 000 Flaschen. Rund um sein Wohnhaus gestaltete Plumb weitere Gebäude aus Flaschen und Zement, darunter den Schiefen Turm von Pisa, das Taj Mahal, einen Brunnen und eine riesige Cola-Flasche. Seine Bauwerke umgab er mit Tierskulpturen aus Beton und gemeißelten Steinen. In den Gärten begrenzen niedrige Mauern verschiedene Blumenbeete mit einem kleinen Wasserfall, Lilien und Fischteichen, einem Totempfahl und einem Miniaturstudio. Nach dem Tod von George Plumb blieben die Besucher aus, und die Anlage verfiel zusehends.

Charpentier à la retraite, **George Plumb** († 1976) acheta un demi-hectare de terre en 1962; dès l'année suivante, il commença à construire son Château de verre. Il bâtit une maisonnette de cinq pièces à partir de bouteilles de toutes sortes, récupérées auprès d'entreprises locales ou données par des voisins. Au fil des ans, il en utilisa plus de 200 000. Autour de l'édifice principal, il érigea une tour de Pise, un Taj Mahal, une bouteille géante de Coca Cola et un puits, tous construits à partir de bouteilles et de ciment. Il y ajouta des animaux en béton ou sculptés dans la pierre, des murets, une petite cascade, des bassins à nénuphars et à poissons, un totem et un petit atelier. Géré comme une simple attraction touristique depuis la mort de Plumb, le site s'est beaucoup dégradé.

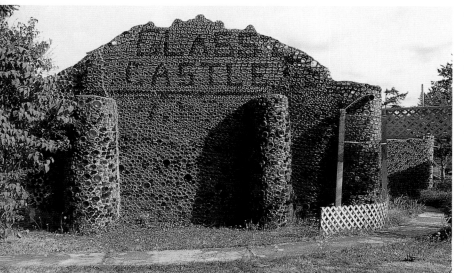

The walls of Plumb's Glass Castle were embellished by sculptures such as an elephant's head, while standing structures included a giant Coca Cola bottle.

Der Kopf eines Elefanten schmückt das Flaschenschloß von George Plumb. Unter den Werken befindet sich auch eine riesige Coca-Cola-Flasche.

Une tête d'éléphant orne les murs du Château de verre bâti par Plumb. Parmi les œuvres isolées se dresse une bouteille de Coca Cola géante.

TheCoralCastle

Homestead, Florida

On the eve of his wedding, **Edward Leedskalnin** (1886–1951) was jilted. In despair, he emigrated from his native Latvia to North America, eventually buying a plot of land in southern Florida in the early Twenties. He mined huge pieces of limestone and carved them into chairs, tables, planets, and a moon and star. He later moved to a ten-acre site, taking all his works with him. Here, he built a walled compound devoted to his lost love, still hoping that she would return to him. Leedskalnin worked alone, carving and moving massive lumps of rock. The stone entrance gates are finely balanced and open at a touch.

Am Abend vor der Hochzeit wurde **Edward Leedskalnin** (1886–1951) von seiner Braut verlassen. In seiner Verzweiflung emigrierte er aus Lettland in die USA und kaufte in den frühen zwanziger Jahren ein Stück Land in Südflorida. Leedskalnin fertigte Stühle, Tische, Planeten, Mond und Sterne aus riesigen Kalksteinblöcken, die er selbst abbaute. Später zog er mit all seinen Skulpturen auf ein vier Hektar großes Gelände um, das er mit Mauern umgab und seiner großen Liebe widmete – immer noch in der Hoffnung, daß sie zu ihm zurückkehren würde. Sowohl den Transport als auch die Bearbeitung der massiven Steine führte Leedskalnin alleine durch. Das steinerne Eingangstor ist optimal ausbalanciert und läßt sich ohne Anstrengungen öffnen.

Abandonné la veille de son mariage, en proie au désespoir, **Edward Leedskalnin** (1886–1951) quitta sa Lettonie natale pour l'Amérique du Nord, où il acheta au début des années vingt un lopin de terre dans le sud de la Floride. Extrayant lui-même du sol d'énormes blocs de calcaire, il sculpta dans le roc des tables, des chaises, des planètes, une lune et une étoile. Lorsqu'il s'installa sur un terrain de quatre hectares, il emporta toutes ses œuvres. A l'abri d'un mur d'enceinte, il créa alors un site consacré à son amour perdu, gardant l'espoir que la femme qu'il aimait lui reviendrait. Il travailla seul, taillant et déplaçant des masses colossales. La barrière d'entrée, en pierre, est si bien conçue qu'une poussée légère suffit à l'ouvrir.

The stone furniture of the Feast of Love table (above) was all hand-hewn by Leedskalnin, as were the stone "Moon Pond" and the massive astrological symbols (following pages) that lie inside the walls.

Die steinernen Stühle um den »Fest der Liebe« genannten Tisch (oben), den steinernen »Moon Pond« und die astrologischen Symbole an der Mauer (folgende Doppelseite) fertigte Leedskalnin selber an.

La table et les sièges en pierre pour le Festin de l'Amour (ci-dessus) ont été entièrement taillés à la main par Leedskalnin, de même que la fontaine «Moon Pond» et d'énormes symboles astrologiques (double page suivante).

140

The reclusive Leedskalnin worked at night behind closed doors, apparently not wanting anyone to see his methods. He planted the compound with lush and exotic foliage.

Der zurückgezogen lebende Leedskalnin arbeitete nachts hinter verschlossenen Türen, um seine Arbeitstechniken geheim zu halten. Er pflanzte auch verschiedene prächtige Bäume und Sträucher.

Solitaire, Leedskalnin travaillait la nuit, enfermé, comme s'il voulait cacher à tous ses méthodes. Il avait aussi planté avec beaucoup de soin une profusion d'arbres et de buissons.

141

MOTHER IN LAW'S CHAIR

THRONE ROOM

TheDes ertSculptu reGarden

Joshua Tree, California

After a working life that encompassed social work and art-teaching, in the late Eighties **Noah Purifoy** (1917–2004) embarked on an artistic career of his own. He has established himself as an artist working with assemblages of found materials in the manner of Edward Kienholz and Robert Rauschenberg, and has exhibited widely both in the United States and abroad. He then moved from Los Angeles to establish an open-air desert studio alongside a trailer home, allowing his creations full rein. By using industrial waste, painted and reclaimed timber, discarded furniture and clothing, he has been able to construct a whole range of large scale tableaux and arrangements, including a giant collage laid out on the ground. The series of sculptures and shelters form an environment wholly at one with the desert landscape.

Bevor **Noah Purifoy** (1917–2004) sich in Los Angeles in den späten achtziger Jahren ganz seiner Tätigkeit als Künstler widmete, hatte er als Sozialarbeiter und Kunstlehrer gearbeitet. Nun gestaltete er Assemblagen aus Fundobjekten im Stil von Edward Kienholz und Robert Rauschenberg und stellte seine Werke international aus. Dann zog er um in einen Wohnwagen in der Wüste und errichtete daneben ein Open-air-Atelier, in dem er seiner Phantasie freien Lauf lassen konnte. Aus Industrieabfall, bemaltem Bauholz, Möbeln vom Sperrmüll und weggeworfenen Kleidern gestaltete er eine Vielzahl an Tableaux und Arrangements, darunter eine riesige Bodencollage. Seine Skulpturen und Hütten bilden ein Visionary Environment, das mit der Wüstenlandschaft verschmilzt.

Tour à tour travailleur social et professeur de disciplines artistiques, **Noah Purifoy** (1917–2004) a pris sa retraite à la fin des années quatre-vingt pour se consacrer à ses propres activités de créateur. Auteur c'assemblages réalisés avec des matériaux de récupération, à la manière d'Edward Kienholz ou de Robert Rauschenberg, il a beaucoup exposé aux Etats-Unis et à l'étranger. Plus tard, il a déménagé de Los Angeles pour installer un atelier à ciel ouvert dans un paysage désertique; il vit dans une caravane tandis que ses œuvres règnent partout alentour. Il a réalisé des compositions de grandes dimensions et même un immense collage au sol, en utilisant des matériaux industriels, du bois de construction peint, du vieux mobilier et des vêtements usagés. Sculptures et abris forment un environnement visionnaire en parfaite harmonie avec le désert alentour.

Purifoy's creations include "Two Similar Belief Systems" (below), a depiction of Christianity and Voodoo, the Curby Express (facing page above), which is mounted on 36 metres of curved track and takes its name from the Kirby vacuum cleaner, and "Shelter" (facing page, below left).

»Two Similar Belief Systems« (unten) stellt Christentum und Voodoo dar. Der Name des »Curby Express« (rechte Seite oben), der auf 36 Metern gebogener Eisenbahnschienen ruht, wurde von einem Kirby-Staubsauger übernommen. Auch »Shelter« (Schutz) gehört zur Purifoys Werken (rechte Seite, unten links).

«Two Similar Belief Systems» (ci-dessous) évoque les systèmes de croyances chrétien et vaudou. Le «Curby Express» (page de droite, en haut), monté sur 36 mètres de rails en courbe, tire son nom des aspirateurs Kirby. Page de droite, en bas à gauche: «Shelter» (abri).

TheDes ertView Tower

Jacumba, California

In 1920, **Bert L. Vaughn** (1878–1974) started building his Desert View Tower as a monument to the early Western pioneers who crossed the desert. The thick-walled, circular three-storey tower was constructed of large blocks of local stone and completed in the Fifties by another builder, Dennis Newman. **MT Radcliffe** (1882–1956), a retired engineer, came to the area for health reasons in the Thirties. He set about carving faces and animals real and mythical into the huge boulders around the Tower. Many of them, especially the powerful skull-like faces, follow the natural shapes and features of the rock, while the lions, snakes and lizards blend easily with the desert landscape. The carvings and statues became known as Boulder Park Caves. Today the Tower is a well-maintained tourist attraction containing a display of artefacts from the old West.

Bert L. Vaughn (1878–1974) errichtete ab 1920 den Desert View Tower als Denkmal für die ersten amerikanischen Siedler. Das dreistöckige Monument besteht aus massiven Steinblöcken aus der Umgebung und wurde in den fünfziger Jahren von dem Architekten Dennis Newman fertiggestellt. Schon in den dreißiger Jahren war der pensionierte Ingenieur **MT Radcliffe** (1882–1956) aus gesundheitlichen Gründen hierhin gezogen, wo er begann, Gesichter, Tiere und mystische Wesen in den Felsen rund um den Desert View Tower zu meißeln. Viele der Darstellungen, besonders die kraftvollen totenkopfähnlichen Gesichter, folgen den natürlichen Formen des Gesteins, während sich die Skulpturen der Löwen, Schlangen und Eidechsen perfekt in die Wüstenlandschaft einfügen. Das Visionary Environment wurde als Boulder Park Caves bekannt, und heute ist der Turm mit den »Reliquien« aus dem Wilden Westen eine bestens instand gehaltene Touristenattraktion.

Bert L. Vaughn (1878–1974) voulait faire de son «Belvédère du désert» un monument à la gloire des premiers pionniers de l'Ouest qui traversèrent le désert. A partir de 1920, il bâtit en gros blocs de pierre du pays une tour ronde de trois étages, aux murs épais, que Dennis Newman acheva plus tard, dans les années cinquante. Quant à **MT Radcliffe** (1882–1956), ingénieur à la retraite, il vint s'installer dans la région au cours des années trente, pour des raisons de santé. Il entreprit de sculpter dans les grands rochers du site des visages, des animaux et des créatures mythiques. Bon nombre de ces œuvres suivent les contours naturels des pierres, en particulier les faces-crânes, tandis que les lions, les serpents et les lézards se fondent dans le paysage désertique. L'ensemble des statues et des bas-reliefs est connu sous le nom de Boulder Park Caves. Attraction touristique bien entretenue, la tour abrite une exposition d'objets et de souvenirs de l'Ouest.

TheDickey villeGrotto

Dickeyville, Wisconsin

The Altar of the Holy Eucharist (above) is one of the several shrines in the Grotto garden. The Tree of Life mosaic (above left) is made of coloured glass. To the right of the imposing entrance to the grotto (facing page) is an American flag sculpture, a symbol of patriotism.

Der Altar des Heiligen Abendmahls (oben) ist einer von vielen Schreinen im Grottengarten. Das Lebensbaummosaik (oben links) besteht aus farbigen Glasscherben. Rechts neben dem beeindruckenden Grotteneingang steht die amerikanische Flagge (rechte Seite).

Le site compte plusieurs petits sanctuaires, parmi lesquels l'autel de l'Eucharistie (ci-dessus). L'Arbre de Vie (en haut à gauche) se compose d'une mosaïque en verre coloré. Un patriotique drapeau américain se dresse à droite de l'entrée imposante (page de droite).

Inspired by Father Dobberstein's Grotto of the Redemption at West Bend (see pages 224–229), **Father Mathias Wernerus** (1873–1931) built the Dickeyville Grotto between 1925 and 1930 with the help and involvement of the local community. It began as a war memorial, but gradually Wernerus' plans became more ambitious. He used local stone and precious minerals alongside broken glass, tiles, crockery and other bits and pieces donated by his parishioners. The imposing entrance, with its mouth-like opening, leads to an intimate and richly ornamented grotto area. The rear of the structure displays a relief of the Tree of Life made of fossilised wood and brightly coloured glass.

Die Grotto of the Redemption in West Bend (siehe Seite 160–163) inspirierte **Father Mathias Wernerus** (1873–1931), zwischen 1925 und 1930 eine eigene Grotte zu bauen, die ursprünglich als Kriegsmahnmal geplant war. Während der Ausführung, bei der ihn seine Gemeinde unterstützte, wurden Wernerus' Pläne immer ehrgeiziger, und es entstand ein Visionary Environment. Für den Bau verwendete er Steine aus dem Umland und wertvolle Mineralien, Glas- und Keramikscherben, Ziegel und andere von den Gemeindemitgliedern gespendete Fundstücke. Der imposante Eingang in Form eines geöffneten Maules führt in die reich mit Ornamenten verzierte Grotte. Im hinteren Teil befindet sich ein Relief des Lebensbaums aus versteinertem Holz und farbenprächtigem Glas.

Inspiré par la Grotte de la Rédemption du père Dobberstein (voir pages 160–163), à West Bend, le **père Mathias Wernerus** (1873–1931) bâtit sa grotte entre 1925 et 1930 avec l'aide des habitants de Dickeyville. D'abord conçu comme un monument aux victimes de la guerre, le projet d'origine se fit plus ambitieux au fil des ans. Le père Wernerus utilisa des pierres du pays et des pierres précieuses mais aussi de la vaisselle cassée, du verre et toutes sortes de matériaux donnés par les paroissiens. L'entrée imposante qui évoque une bouche mène à une grotte secrète ornée à profusion. Dehors, à l'arrière de l'édifice, s'élève un Arbre de Vie en bois fossilisé et en verre de couleurs vives.

Fore ver tron

Lodi, Wisconsin

Tom O. Every (*1939) worked in industrial salvage. He came to appriciate the beauty of factory machinery and collected over a thousand tons of unwanted industrial plant. In 1983, he passed the salvage business on to his son, and devoted himself to constructing an environment of massive machine components. He transformed himself into Dr Evermor and named his construction "Forevertron", a fantastical device for space travel. On the summit of the machine, a glass ball inside a copper egg waits to shoot Dr Evermor into space through a magnetic lightning beam. At the northern end, a vast telescope, constructed of tubes and wheels, points skywards. The whole environment weighs 300 tons; it is 35 metres wide by 15 metres high. Among its components are elements from paper mills, breweries, power plants, agricultural machinery, machine shops and even a decontamination chamber from the Apollo Space Mission.

A giant Eagle's head under construction and a flamingo are part of Dr Evermor's "Bird Bond" series.

Ein Flamingo und ein gigantischer Adlerkopf, der noch im Bau befindlich ist, gehören zur »Bird Band«-Reihe von Dr. Evermor.

Docteur Evermor crée des séries d'oiseaux, dont cette tête d'aigle géante, en cours de construction, et ce flamant.

Vor seiner Pensionierung betrieb **Tom O. Every** (*1939) eine Firma, die Industrieanlagen demontierte. Im Lauf der Zeit entdeckte er die Schönheit von Maschinen und sammelte tonnenweise Industrieschrott. Schließlich übergab er 1983 die Firma seinem Sohn und begann mit der Errichtung eines phantastischen Weltraumtransporters aus gewaltigen Maschinenbestandteilen. Er nannte sich Dr. Evermor und bezeichnete seine Konstruktion als »Forevertron«. Auf der Spitze des Apparates befindet sich in einem Kupferei eine Glaskugel, mit der sich Dr. Evermor durch einen magnetischen Blitzstrahl ins All schießen lassen kann. Am nördlichen Ende ragt ein gewaltiges Teleskop aus Reifen und Rohren in den Himmel. Die 300 Tonnen schwere, 35 Meter breite und 15 Meter hohe Konstruktion besteht aus ausrangierten Maschinenteilen aus Papierfabriken, Brauereien, Kraftwerken, der Landwirtschaft und sogar einer Dekontaminierungskammer des Apollo-Raumfahrtprogramms.

Propriétaire d'une entreprise de récupération de matériel d'usine, **Tom O. Every** (*1939) découvrit la beauté des machines industrielles en les manipulant. Il mit de côté plus d'un millier de tonnes de rebuts. Lorsqu'il laissa l'affaire à son fils en 1983, il se transforma en Dr. Evermor et se consacra à la création d'un environnement d'éléments énormes, baptisé «Forevertron», base fantastique pour d'hypothétiques missions spatiales. Un engin surmonté d'un œuf en cuivre abritant une sphère en verre se tient prêt à propulser le maître des lieux dans l'espace, à l'aide d'un rayon magnétique. A l'extrémité nord, un imposant téléscope, fait de roues et de tubes, pointe vers le ciel. L'ensemble pèse 300 tonnes, mesure 35 mètres de largeur et 15 de hauteur. Les éléments proviennent de papeteries, de brasseries, de centrales électriques, d'ateliers d'usinage et de machines agricoles; à signaler enfin, un sas de décontamination de la mission Apollo.

TheGardenof Eden

Lucas, Kansas

Starting in 1905, **Samuel Perry Dinsmoor** (1843–1932) built his house in log-cabin style using hewn limestone. Around it, between 1908 and 1929, he constructed his Garden of Eden, which features 30 concrete trees connected by sinuous branches and holding over 150 cement figures reflecting his religious and political beliefs. The tableaux include the "Crucifixion of Labor" by a doctor, lawyer, banker and preacher, and "Cain and Abel", a combination of biblical and political allegory. An array of birds and beasts is topped by the brightly painted Stars and Stripes. Dinsmoor, who married a 21-year-old at the age of 89, lies buried in a glass-topped coffin in a mausoleum in the Garden.

Photo: Courtesy of Garden of Eden Inc.

Samuel Perry Dinsmoor (1843–1932) gestaltete sein Eigenheim aus Kalksteinblöcken im Stil eines Blockhauses und errichtete zwischen 1908 und 1929 in seinem Garten 30 Betonbäume. An den gewundenen Ästen hängen mehr als 150 Zementstatuen, die Dinsmoors religiöse und politische Überzeugungen widerspiegeln. Eine Szene zeigt die »Kreuzigung der Arbeit« durch einen Arzt, Rechtsanwalt, Banker und Priester, eine andere die biblisch-politische Allegorie »Kain und Abel«. Eine farbenprächtige amerikanische Flagge krönt ein Arrangement aus Vögeln und Tieren. Mit 89 Jahren heiratete Dinsmoor eine 21jährige Frau, starb und wurde in seinem Garten in einem Mausoleum beigesetzt – in einem Sarg mit gläsernem Deckel.

Samuel Perry Dinsmoor (1843–1932) bâtit une demeure imitant les traditionnelles maisons en rondins avec des pierres taillées dans le calcaire. Tout autour, il érigea entre 1908 et 1929 son Jardin d'Eden avec 30 arbres de béton où perchent plus de 150 créatures en ciment reflétant ses convictions religieuses et politiques. Parmi les scènes représentées figurent la «Crucifixion du travail» par un médecin, un juriste, un banquier et un pasteur; ou encore une allégorie biblique et politique intitulée «Caïn et Abel». La bannière étoilée domine tout un peuple d'animaux. Dinsmoor épousa à 89 ans une femme de 21 ans. A sa mort, il fut enterré dans un cercueil à couvercle de verre, placé dans un mausolée du jardin.

Samuel Perry Dinsmoor surrounded his limestone Log Cabin Home with biblical figures, among them Cain and his wife (above right), and Abel's body being discovered by his wife (left). Two storks hold unborn children beneath their wings (above left), while behind them a guardian angel stands beneath God's all-seeing eye.

Samuel Perry Dinsmoor umgab sein Steinhaus, das im Stil eines Holzhauses gebaut ist, mit biblischen Figuren, darunter Kain und seine Frau (oben rechts) sowie Abels Frau, die die Leiche ihres Mannes entdeckt (links). Zwei Störche tragen ungeborene Kinder unter ihren Flügeln (oben links). Dahinter erhebt sich ein Schutzengel unter dem allwissenden Auge Gottes.

Autour de sa demeure de pierre imitant une maison en rondins, Samuel Perry Dinsmoor a installé une foule de figures bibliques, parmi lesquelles Caïn et sa femme (ci-dessus à droite), la femme d'Abel découvrant le corps de son mari (à gauche). Deux cigognes portent des enfants à naître sous leurs ailes (ci-dessus à gauche), tandis que derrière elles se dresse un ange gardien, à côté de l'œil de Dieu auquel rien n'échappe.

TheGrotto oftheRede mption

West Bend, Iowa

Inspired by the European tradition of holy grottoes and shrines, **Father Paul Dobberstein** (1872–1954) built his magnificent Grotto from stone, rocks, boulders, exotic minerals and fossilised wood, travelling thousands of miles in his search for minerals with which to embellish it. With the aid of local people and one full-time helper, Matt Szerensce, who devoted his whole working life to the Grotto, Dobberstein created a complex of seven shrines illustrating the story of the Redemption (1912–1959). The path that links them leads past smaller shrines representing the Stations of the Cross. Specially commissioned marble statues from Italy were set into the separate grottoes, their smooth finish contrasting with the richly textured décor glittering with agate and quartz. The entrance is encrusted with minerals and topped by the figure of Christ. Much of the construction was carried out with specially prefabricated slabs of concrete, into which stones and minerals were embedded as they dried. The Grotto became a famous place of pilgrimage, and Dobberstein went on to construct a lake for fishing or skating, a small zoo and a restaurant. A master grotto-builder, Dobberstein created almost a dozen other grottoes and monuments in the mid-West, and inspired others to build their own.

Father Paul Dobberstein (1872–1954) errichtete die Grotto of the Redemption (1912–1959) nach dem Vorbild heiliger Grotten und Schreine in Europa aus Steinen, Felsblöcken, exotischen Mineralien und versteinertem Holz. Auf der Suche nach Mineralien für die Höhlendekoration legte er mehrere tausend Kilometer zurück. Bei dem Bau wurde er von Anwohnern und besonders von Matt Szerensce unterstützt, der sein ganzes Leben lang an der Grotte arbeitete. Dobberstein errichtete einen Komplex aus sieben Schreinen mit Darstellungen aus dem Buch der Richter sowie einen kleinen Pfad mit Kreuzwegstationen. In separaten Höhlen sind italienische Marmorstatuen aufgestellt, deren glatte Oberfläche mit den schimmernden Quarz- und Achatwänden kontrastieren.

Über dem Eingang, den Dobberstein mit Mineralien auslegte, thront eine Christusfigur. Ein Großteil der Anlage besteht aus vorgefertigten Betonplatten, in die während des Trocknens Steine und Mineralien eingelassen wurden. Die Höhle wurde zu einem beliebten Wallfahrtsort mit verschiedenen Attraktionen, wie einem See zum Angeln und Eislaufen, einem kleinen Tierpark und einem Restaurant. Dobberstein war ein Meister des Höhlenbaus: Er errichtete zwölf weitere Höhlen und Monumente im mittleren Westen der USA und inspirierte viele Visionary-Environment-Künstler.

Puisant dans la tradition européenne des grottes sacrées et des sanctuaires, le **père Paul Dobberstein** (1872–1954) édifia à West Bend un magnifique ensemble de petits édifices. Utilisant des pierres, des rochers, des minéraux insolites et du bois fossilisé, il parcourut des milliers de kilomètres à la recherche de ces matériaux. Avec l'aide des gens du pays et d'un assistant à plein temps, Matt Szerensce, qui travailla toute sa vie sur le site, Dobberstein créa sept chapelles illustrant l'histoire de la Rédemption (1912–1959), reliées par un chemin bordé de structures plus petites représentant les stations de la Croix. Les grottes abritent des statues de marbre commandées en Italie, dont le poli contraste avec les surfaces à la riche texture où brillent des agathes et des quartz. Un Christ surmonte le portail incrusté de pierres. L'essentiel des constructions fut réalisé en dalles de béton coulées sur place et piquées de pierres avant d'avoir séché. Le site devint un lieu de pèlerinage célèbre et Dobberstein y ajouta un lac pour la pêche ou le patin à glace en hiver, un petit zoo et un restaurant. Maître dans son art, il bâtit près d'une douzaine de grottes et de monuments dans le Middle West et en inspira bien d'autres.

The pillars and Stations of the Cross are covered with precious stones, mosaics, brown jasper, and fine crystals. Father Dobberstein used the circle to symbolize God's unending work redeeming the world. The Grotto has the largest collection of cut and polished agates in the world. The archway to the right of the Northern side of the grotto leads to the Stations of the Cross (see page 160). In the Grotto of the Ten Commandments stands a statue of Moses, surrounded by hand-made rosettes of precious stones and crystals (see page 161).

Die Pfeiler und Kreuzwegstationen sind mit Edelsteinen, Mosaiken, braunem Jaspis und Kristallglas bedeckt. Der Kreis symbolisiert die Unendlichkeit von Gottes Schöpfung. Die Grotte verfügt über die größte Achatsammlung der Welt. Durch den Bogen rechts von der Nordseite der Grotte erreicht man die Kreuzwegstationen (siehe Seite 160). In der Grotte der Zehn Gebote wird die Statue von Moses gerahmt von handgefertigten Edelstein- und Kristallglasrosetten (siehe Seite 161).

Les piliers et les autels sont couverts de pierres précieuses, de mosaïques, de jaspe brun, de cristaux. On retrouve un peu partout le cercle, qui symbolisait aux yeux du père Dobberstein l'œuvre sans fin de Dieu pour le salut du monde. Le site abrite la plus grande collection mondiale d'agathes. L'arche juste à droite de la façade nord de la grotte mène aux stations de la Croix (voir page 160). Dans la Grotte des dix commandements se dresse la statue de Moïse, entourée de rosaces en pierres précieuses et en cristaux (voir page 161).

The Heidel berg Project

Detroit, Michigan

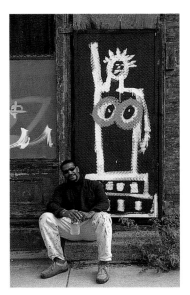

Tyree Guyton (*1955), initially helped by his wife Karen and his grandfather Sam Mackey, has transformed a decaying area of Detroit. Using rubbish and larger objects abandoned in the streets, former art student Guyton has, since 1986, decorated abandoned buildings with quantities of shoes, telephones, clocks, old bicycles, soft toys, broken dolls, clothing, signs and paintings. The effect is disconcertingly bizarre and brings colour and life to a drab environment. Guyton has waged a constant battle with the city authorities, who wish to return the mean streets of Detroit to their depressing original state, and his work has often been dismantled or torn down. Yet Guyton started again each time.

Tyree Guyton (*1955) verwandelte mit Hilfe seiner Frau Karen und seines Großvaters Sam Mackey ein graues, heruntergekommenes Viertel von Detroit in ein bizarres Visionary Environment. Der ehemalige Kunststudent dekorierte ab 1986 verlassene Gebäude mit alten Schuhen, Telefonen, Uhren, Fahrrädern, Stofftieren, Puppen, Kleidungsstücken, Schildern und Gemälden, die er im Müll oder auf den Straßen fand. Die Behörden ließen seine Werke regelmäßig demontieren und Tyree Guyton mußte jedes Mal wieder von vorne anfangen.

Aidé au départ par sa femme Karen et son grand-père Sam Mackey, **Tyree Guyton** (*1955) a complètement transformé une zone de Detroit laissée à l'abandon. A partir de 1986, l'ancien étudiant en art a décoré des bâtiments désaffectés avec ses propres peintures ainsi qu'avec des objets récupérés dans les rues alentour: chaussures, téléphones, horloges, vieilles bicyclettes, jouets en peluche, poupées cassées, vêtements, panneaux et enseignes. L'ensemble produit un effet bizarre, discordant, qui donne des couleurs et de la vie à un quartier désolé. Guyton est en lutte permanente avec la municipalité qui veut rendre les rues à leur grisaille habituelle et, bien souvent, ses travaux furent démontés ou démolis. Pourtant, chaque fois, Guyton les a reconstruits.

The famous Polka Dot House (above) was surrounded by various works of art. The O. J. House or Obstruction of Justice House (right and facing page) was adorned with found objects.

Kunstwerke umgaben das berühmte Polka Dot House (oben). Das O. J. House oder »Haus der Behinderung der Gerechtigkeit« (rechts und rechte Seite) zierten Fundobjekte.

La célèbre Polka Dot House (ci-dessus) était entourée d'œuvres variées. La O. J. House, ou Maison de l'obstruction à la justice (à droite et page de droite), était ornée d'objets trouvés.

TheJu nkCastle

Whitman County, Washington

Former art teacher **Vic Moore** (*1926) began work on his junk building in the Sixties and he and his wife **Bobbie** (*1931) moved there soon after they were married. Made of old car panels, washing machine parts, railway sleepers, machine housings and reclaimed sheet metal, the turreted castle stands alone in the landscape, fitting snugly into the contours of the hill on which it is built. Old car windows and the glass of washing machine doors let light into the rusting structure which also acted as Moore's workshop and studio for making his metal assemblages and figures. The Moores recently sold the building and attempts are being made to declare it a historical landmark.

Né en 1926, professeur enseignant des disciplines artistiques, **Vic Moore** (*1926) a commencé à créer sa maison de ferraille dans les années soixante; il s'y est installé peu après son mariage avec **Bobbie** (*1931). Composé de panneaux de carrosserie, d'éléments de machines à laver, de traverses, de coques de machines et de plaques de métal récupérées, son château à tourelles adossé à une colline se dresse, solitaire, dans le paysage. Des fenêtres de voitures et des hublots de machines à laver laissent entrer la lumière dans cette architecture rouillée qui abritait l'atelier où Moore créait ses sculptures et ses assemblages métalliques. Le couple a vendu la maison récemment. Il est question d'en faire un site protégé.

Der ehemalige Kunstlehrer **Vic Moore** (*1926) begann in den sechziger Jahren mit dem Bau seines Trödelhauses. Kurz nach der Hochzeit konnte er mit seiner Frau **Bobbie** (*1931) einziehen. Das mit Türmen verzierte Haus aus alten Eisenbahnschwellen, Metallplatten und Teilen aus Autokarosserien, Waschmaschinen sowie Haushaltsgeräten erhebt sich einsam auf einem Hügel über die umliegende Landschaft. Durch alte Windschutzscheiben und Waschmaschinentüren dringt Licht in das rostige Gebilde, das gleichzeitig als Atelier-Werkstatt diente, in der Moore seine Metallskulpturen und -assemblagen anfertigte. Kürzlich haben die Moores das Trödelhaus verkauft, das wahrscheinlich zum Denkmal erklärt werden wird.

MaryNohl's

Fox Point, Wisconsin

Mary Nohl (1914–2001) started circa 1928 to create a sculpture environment beside her home on the shores of Lake Michigan. The large scale figures and huge heads that she has made from cement and local stone create a very striking impression. She has also carved figures from tree trunks. The walls of her house are decorated with driftwood figures and wooden patterns. The brightly painted and patterned interior, with windows stained in bold colours, contains hundreds of mixed media works. Though she had suffered over the years from local prejudice and vandalism, Mary Nohl had continued with her work undaunted. Today, the Kohler Foundation Inc. is making an effort to document and preserve her art.

Ab 1928 errichtete **Mary Nohl** (1914–2001) neben ihrem Haus am Ufer des Lake Michigan ein Visionary Environment. Die überdimensionalen Skulpturen und Köpfe bestehen aus Zement und Steinen aus dem Umland, außerdem schnitzte Mary Nohl auch Figuren aus Baumstämmen. Die Fassade ihres Hauses versah sie mit Ornamenten und Gestalten aus Treibholz, während in die Fenster farbenprächtige Buntglasscheiben eingesetzt wurden. Die reiche Innendekoration setzt sich aus zahllosen Kunstwerken der verschiedensten Gattungen in kühnen Mustern und Farben zusammen. Obwohl Mary Nohl mit Vorurteilen und Vandalismus konfrontiert wurde, hatte sie die Courage, ihre Arbeit fortzusetzen. Heute kümmert sich die Kohler Foundation Inc. um die Erhaltung und Dokumentation des Environment.

Mary Nohl (1914–2001) a commencé en 1928 à aménager un environnement autour de sa maison, sur les rives du lac Michigan. Utilisant la pierre locale et du ciment, elle l'a peuplé de grandes figures et de visages immenses, qui sont autant de présences impressionnantes. Elle a également realisé des personnages à partir de troncs d'arbres et orné les murs de la maison de personnages en bois flotté et de motifs décoratifs, en bois également. L'intérieur, peint de dessins aux couleurs vives, abrite des centaines de ses œuvres, baignées par les couleurs audacieuses des vitres. Mal vue par ses voisins, victime d'actes de vandalisme, Mary Nohl avait cependant eu le courage de poursuivre son œuvre. Aujourd' hui la Kohler Foundation Inc. conserve l'environnement et rassemble toute la documentation la concernant.

Photo: Ron Byers

Mary Nohl's front yard contains scores of sculptures made from concrete, stones, glass, and wood, depicting a variety of figures and beasts.

Im Vorgarten von Mary Nohl befinden sich Skulpturen aus Zement, Stein, Glas und Holz, die verschiedenste Gestalten und Tiere darstellen.

La cour de Mary Nohl abrite une foule de sculptures en ciment, en pierre, en verre et en bois, représentant des hommes et des animaux.

Oisea uxChaus seGros

Beauce, Canada

La Maison des enfants (The Children's house) was built by Richard Greaves in September 1995 (below).

La Maison des enfants (das Haus der Kinder) wurde von Richard Greaves im September 1995 errichtet (unten).

La Maison des enfants a été construite par Richard Greaves en septembre 1995 (ci-desscus).

A former chef and graphic designer, **Richard Greaves** (*1952) took himself off to the woods with a group of friends at a village in Quebec in 1982. Using reclaimed materials he has created a several hundred assemblage sculptures, both large and small in scale. Eventually he was led to construct a collection of shacks and shelters in the woods. Each is built of rescued junk materials – old tyres, bicycles, window frames, machine parts – and constructed around a central stove which gives a welcoming warmth to visitors who come to stay, relax, think and work.

Der ehemalige Koch und Grafikdesigner **Richard Greaves** (*1952) zog 1982 mit einigen Freunden in die Wälder von Kanada, wo sie sich in einem kleinen Ort nahe Quebec ansiedelten. Hier gestaltete Greaves mitten im Wald aus verschiedenen Altmaterialien einige hundert kleinere und größere Skulpturen sowie eine Gruppe von Hütten und Unterständen. Dabei verwendete er unter anderem ausgediente Reifen, Fahrräder, Fensterrahmen und Maschinenteile. Die Gebäude sind rund um einen Ofen angeordnet, der die Besucher zum Verweilen, Erholen, Nachdenken und Arbeiten einlädt.

Cuisinier et designer graphique, **Richard Greaves** (*1952) est parti s'installer avec des amis dans un village du Québec, en 1982. Il a créé plusieurs centaines d'assemblages, grands et petits, à base de matériaux de récupération. Puis il a construit dans les bois des cabanes et des abris, avec de vieux pneus, des bicyclettes, des cadres de fenêtre, des pièces mécaniques. Au centre de chaque hutte, un poêle offre sa chaleur réconfortante aux gens qui viennent ici pour se reposer, réfléchir ou travailler.

Richard used to cook water in La Maison d'Emilie (right) to make maple syrup. Nearby is La Tapisserie which serves as a toilet (below). He used reclaimed material to decorate La Maison des enfants (bottom right) and La Maison d'Emilie (following pages).

In La Maison d'Emilie (rechts) kochte Greaves früher Wasser, um Ahornsirup zuzubereiten. Ganz in der Nähe befindet sich La Tapisserie, die als Toilettenhaus fungiert (unten). Für die Dekoration von La Maison des enfants (unten rechts) und La Maison d'Emilie (folgende Doppelseite) verwendete der Künstler ausschließlich Altmaterialien.

Dans la Maison d'Emilie (à droite), Richard Greaves fait bouillir de l'eau pour préparer du sirop d'érable. Tout à côté se dresse La Tapisserie (ci-dessous), qui sert de salle de bains. Il a décoré la Maison des enfants (en bas à droite) et la Maison d'Emilie (double page suivante) avec des matériaux récupérés.

The Paradise Garden

Summerville, Georgia

The most famous of American folk artists, **Reverend Howard Finster** (1916–2001), "man of visions", made his living by repairing bicycles, lawnmowers and televisions. On his retirement in 1965, he took to preaching the gospel in paint and form. Cement walls and walkways embedded with stones, glass, pottery fragments and discarded tools, lead to buildings constructed of bottles, mirrors and reclaimed materials, including the four-storey World's Folk Art Church. A tower of old bicycles, a tree of hubcaps and a giant shoe are surrounded by sculptures, paintings and unusual found objects. All around stand evangelical messages and Biblical quotations on bright hand-painted signs. Finster has completed over 35 000 individual artworks, all numbered and dated. The garden is now maintained by friends and followers of the Reverend, and unfortunately many original pieces, some of them on a large scale, have been sold and removed.

Der berühmteste Vertreter der amerikanischen »Folk Art« war **Reverend Howard Finster** (1916–2001), der ursprünglich Fahrrad- und Fernsehmechaniker war und dann als »Man of Visions« das Evangelium predigte. 1965 begann er mit der Errichtung des Gartens, in dem mit Steinen, Glas, Keramikscherben und ausrangierten Werkzeugen ausgelegte Betonwege zu Gebäuden aus Flaschen, Spiegeln und Altmaterialien führen. Hier befindet sich auch die vierstöckige World's Folk Art Church. Skulpturen, Gemälde und ungewöhnliche Fundobjekte umgeben einen Turm aus Fahrrädern, einen Baum aus Radkappen sowie einen überdimensionalen Schuh. Und überall finden sich leuchtende Schilder mit handschriftlichen Bibelzitaten und Botschaften aus dem Evangelium. Finster fertigte mehr als 35 000 Einzelkunstwerke an, die er alle numerierte und datierte. Heute wird Paradise Garden von Freunden und Anhängern des Reverends instand gehalten. Viele seiner Originalwerke, darunter auch einige größere Stücke, wurden inzwischen leider verkauft.

Le **révérend Howard Finster** (1916–2001), «homme de visions», est le représentant le plus célèbre du «folk art» américain. Ayant cessé ses activités de réparateur de bicyclettes, de tondeuses et de télévisions, il entreprit de prêcher l'évangile au moyen de l'art. Dans son Jardin paradis, commencé en 1965, des chemins et des murs en ciment incrusté de pierres, de tessons et d'outils divers, relient des édifices construits à partir de bouteilles, de miroirs et de matériaux récupérés, comme l'Eglise mondiale du folk art, haute de quatre étages. Une tour de vieilles bicyclettes, un arbre d'enjoliveurs, une chaussure géante se mêlent à des sculptures, des peintures et des objets étranges. Des pancartes ponctuent l'ensemble de messages évangéliques et de citations bibliques. Finster a réalisé 35 000 œuvres, datées et numérotées. Aujourd'hui le jardin est entretenu par des amis et admirateurs du révérend; de nombreuses pièces, dont certaines de grandes dimensions, ont été vendues.

A giant boot lies outside one of Finster's earlier buildings while the four-storey World's Folk Art Church (facing page) climbs above the garden.

Ein überdimensionaler Schuh vor Finsters früheren Bauwerken. Die vierstöckige World's Folk Art Church (rechte Seite) erhebt sich über Finsters Garten.

Une bottine géante s'appuie contre l'une des premières constructions de Finster. L'Eglise mondiale du folk art (page de droite) domine le jardin du haut de ses quatre étages.

Pas aquan

Buena Vista, Georgia

A fortune teller and mystic, **Eddie Owens Martin** (1908–1986), known as St EOM, returned to his childhood home in Georgia in the Fifties and, between 1958 and 1985, transformed this four-acre smallholding into a temple compound dedicated to his one-man religion of Pasaquoyanism. The Land of Pasaquan is a series of temples and pavilions enclosed by brightly painted walls and totems. The entrance is flanked by large figures of a man and a woman wearing openwork green "levitation suits". St EOM's imagery was strongly influenced by the religious iconography of the East, with mandalas, yin-yang symbols and oriental decoration interspersed among the powerful faces and figures. The building interiors are richly decorated with murals and mandalas. St EOM supported himself by telling fortunes, for which he dressed in colourful flowing robes – the regalia of the high priest of Pasaquan. Since his death the site has been maintained by the Pasaquan Society.

Der Wahrsager und Mystiker **Eddie Owens Martin** (1908–1986), der auch als St. EOM bekannt ist, kehrte in den fünfziger Jahren in sein Elternhaus nach Georgia zurück und baute zwischen 1958 und 1985 den 1,5 Hektar großen Hof zu einem Tempel des »Pasaquoyanism« aus. Der Hohepriester dieser Einmannreligion wurde von Martin persönlich verkörpert. St. EOM gestaltete mehrere Tempel und Pavillons, die er mit bunten Mauern und Totems umgab. Zwei große weibliche und männliche Gestalten in offenen grünen »Levitationsgewändern« flankieren den Eingang. Die fernöstlichen Religionen übten eine starke Faszination auf Martin aus, was sich in Mandalas, Yin-und-Yang-Symbolen sowie orientalischen Ornamenten zeigt. Innen sind die Gebäude aufwendig verziert. St. EOM inszenierte sich selbst in farbenprächtigen Roben als Wahrsager und Hohepriester von Pasaquan. Seit seinem Tod ist die Anlage im Besitz der Pasaquan Society.

Diseur de bonne aventure et mystique, **Eddie Owens Martin** (1908–1986), dit saint EOM, retrouva la maison de son enfance dans les années cinquante. Il transforma la petite propriété de 1,5 hectare entre 1958 et 1985 en un haut lieu du «pasaquoyanisme», sa religion personnelle. La Terre de Pasaquan se couvrit de temples et de pavillons, protégés par des murs et des totems imposants peints de couleurs vives. A l'entrée, se dressent deux grands personnages, masculin et féminin, vêtus de «costumes de lévitation» verts, laissant voir le corps à certains endroits. Saint EOM puisa ses motifs décoratifs dans l'iconographie religieuse orientale (mandalas, symboles du yin et du yang, ornements). Peintures murales et mandalas décorent l'intérieur des édifices. Le créateur gagnait sa vie en prédisant l'avenir, vêtu d'une ample robe de couleur vive, tel le grand prêtre de Pasaquan. Depuis sa mort, le site est géré par la Pasaquan Society.

A small pagoda located near the rear section conceals St EOM's gas tanks (facing page). The Dancing Muses in the interior of the Oratory (above top), rarely seen during St EOM's lifetime, symbolise aspects of creativity. A pagoda built around a well houses an upper level studio (above). St EOM claimed that his spirit would reside here until his next incarnation.

Eine kleine Pagode verbirgt die Gastanks von St. EOM (linke Seite). Die Tanzenden Musen im Inneren des Oratoriums (ganz oben), das zu St. EOMs Lebzeiten nur selten zugänglich war, stehen für verschiedene Aspekte der Kreativität. In der oberen Etage der über einem Brunnen errichteten Pagode (oben) befindet sich ein Atelier. St. EOM behauptete, daß sein Geist hier bis zur seiner nächsten Reinkarnation verbleiben würde.

Une petite pagode au fond du terrain dissimule les cuves à mazout (page de gauche). Peu de gens connaissaient, du vivant de saint EOM, les Muses dansantes (tout en haut) qui peuplent l'oratoire et symbolisent la créativité. La pagode construite autour d'un puits (ci-dessus) abrite un atelier, situé au premier étage; saint EOM prétendait que son esprit demeurerait en ce lieu jusqu'à sa prochaine réincarnation.

LasPozas

Xilitla, Mexico

English aristocrat **Edward James** (1907–1984) was a poet and a patron of the Surrealists. He came across the remote village of Xilitla on a trip to Mexico in 1945 and fell in love with the isolated site and rich vegetation. He bought 2 500 acres of steep jungle land as a plantation for coffee, oranges and orchids, and installed a manager and staff. After many visits to the area, he moved down from California and began in 1962 to build his Surrealist palace among the exotic foliage. Employing a workforce of up to 70, he grew totally absorbed in his project, directing the construction from dawn to dusk, and expanding his plans as time went on. The complex's flowing forms were constructed by local carpenters making curved wooden shuttering to hold the setting concrete. Immensely strong, the thick walls and sturdy floors of the main house should ensure its longevity. It is surrounded by temples, stairways, fountains and arcades in their dramatic setting among the waterfalls of the hilly landscape. James died before his great project could be completed; he had always felt that an unfinished state was its destiny. He liked to think of it as an archeological mystery for the future.

1945 entdeckte der englische Aristokrat **Edward James** (1907–1984), Dichter und Anhänger des Surrealismus, bei einem Kurzurlaub in Mexiko das entlegene Dorf Xilitla. Er war augenblicklich fasziniert und erwarb 1 000 Hektar Dschungelland, auf dem er mit einem Manager und mehreren Hilfskräften Kaffee-, Orangen- und Orchideenplantagen anlegte. Bevor der Dichter endgültig nach Mexiko übersiedelte, pendelte er zwischen Kalifornien und seinen Plantagen. Inmitten der exotischen Flora errichtete Edward James ab 1962 einen surrealistischen Palast, für dessen Bau er 70 Hilfskräfte beschäftigte. Die Arbeiten begannen im Morgengrauen und wurden bis in die Nacht fortgesetzt. James erstellte keinerlei Pläne für sein Projekt, sondern traf alle Entscheidungen intuitiv. Mexikanische Schreiner entwarfen fließende Formen für die Holzverkleidung des Bauwerkes. Das mächtige Hauptgebäude mit dicken Mauern und starken Fundamenten, die umliegenden Tempel, Treppen, Springbrunnen und Arkaden wurden zwischen den Wasserfällen und Hügeln des mexikanischen Hochlandes dramatisch in Szene gesetzt. Gewaltige Säulen tragen Kapitelle in Form von massiven Blumenblättern, die von farbenprächtigem Zement bekrönt werden. Edward James war stets der Meinung, sein Bauwerk solle unvollendet bleiben, und tatsächlich starb er vor der Fertigstellung. Der Gedanke, ein archäologisches Rätsel für künftige Generationen geschaffen zu haben, hätte ihm sicherlich gefallen.

Aristocrate, poète et mécène des surréalistes, l'Anglais **Edward James** (1907–1984) découvrit en 1945 le village isolé de Xilitla: il tomba sous le charme de sa solitude et de sa riche végétation. Il acheta 1 000 hectares de terrain vallonné envahi par la jungle, pour en faire une plantation de caféiers, d'orangers et d'orchidées; il embaucha un intendant et du personnel. Après de nombreux séjours sur place, il quitta la Californie, s'installa à Xilitla et commença à construire à partir de 1962 un palais surréaliste noyé dans la verdure. Employant jusqu'à 70 personnes, travaillant de l'aube au crépuscule, il s'absorba totalement dans sa tâche, agrandissant le projet selon l'inspiration du moment. Des charpentiers locaux fabriquèrent les caissons en bois où le béton était moulé en formes douces et fluides. D'une solidité à toute épreuve avec leurs murs épais et leurs sols très résistants, la demeure principale, les temples, les escaliers, les fontaines et les arcades forment un décor

spectaculaire sur les pentes où s'élancent des chutes d'eau. Les grosses colonnes surmontées de chapiteaux en forme de pétales sont recouvertes de ciment aux couleurs vives. James mourut avant d'avoir terminé son œuvre, un inachèvement qu'il avait toujours pressenti: il aimait à croire que Xilitla constituerait un mystère archéologique pour les générations à venir.

Giant columns, inspired by the shapes of flowers and plants, stand amid the lush jungle foliage.

Riesige Säulen, deren Formen an Blüten und Blätter erinnern, ragen im Dschungel empor.

D'énormes colonnes aux formes végétales se dressent dans la jungle luxuriante.

The Prairie Moon Sculpture Garden and Museum

Cochrane, Wisconsin

Bored in his retirement, farmer **Herman Rusch** (1885–1985) opened a museum to display his collection of souvenirs and natural oddities. Using barrel hoops as armatures, in 1958 he built his first structure: a wall of interconnecting concrete arches. Each of the supporting pillars was topped with a conical spire. Coloured glass, pebbles, pieces of mirror and broken pottery were inlaid into the wet cement, which was tinted with red dye. Rusch was active till 1974, building a birdhouse, a small Hindu temple, a watchtower and two tall sun spires topped with mirrored stars. His sculptures include two dinosaurs and a giant stone cactus.

Nachdem der Farmer **Herman Rusch** (1885–1985) sich auf das Altenteil zurückgezogen hatte, eröffnete er ein Museum für seine Sammlung von Souvenirs und Kuriositäten. Rusch errichtete 1958 zunächst eine Mauer aus miteinander verbundenen Zementarkaden, die er mit einem Beschlag aus Faßreifen dekorierte. Er färbte den nassen Zement rot ein und legte ihn mit Buntglas, Kieselsteinen, Spiegel- und Keramikscherben aus. Bis 1974 gestaltete Rusch Pflanzenkübel, ein Vogelhaus, einen kleinen Hindutempel, einen Wachturm und zwei Sonnentürme mit gläsernen Sternen auf der Spitze. Zu seinen Skulpturen zählen zwei Dinosaurier und ein überdimensionaler Steinkaktus.

Agriculteur, **Herman Rusch** (1885–1985) ne supporta pas le désœuvrement de la retraite; il décida donc d'ouvrir un musée pour exposer sa collection de souvenirs et de curiosités naturelles. Puis, en 1958, il bâtit une première structure, une enfilade d'arcs ayant pour armature des cercles de torneaux; il orna chaque pilier d'un clocheton et incrusta dans le ciment teint en rouge du verre coloré, des galets, des éclats de miroir et de la vaisselle cassée. Rusch poursuivit son travail jusqu'en 1974, aménageant des jardinières, une volière, un petit temple hindou, une tour de guet et deux flèches surmontées d'étoiles en miroir. Citons parmi ses sculptures deux dinosaures et un cactus géant en pierre.

The artist's self-portrait gazes at his sculpture garden (above left). A gracefully arched fence, built in just one year, runs over 80 metres.

Das Selbstporträt des Künstlers blickt über den Skulpturengarten (oben links). Der anmutig geschwungene, mehr als 80 Meter lange Zaun wurde in nur einem Jahr errichtet.

Rusch s'est représenté lui-même, veillant sur son jardin (en haut à gauche). Une gracieuse barrière à arcades, construite en un an, court sur plus de 80 mètres.

184

TheSal vation Moun tain

Niland, California

Leonard Knight (*1931) spent five years in Nebraska sewing together a hot air balloon bearing the words "God Is Love". The balloon grew so big, 100 metres high, that he was never able to get it off the ground. In 1986, he drove to the Mojave Desert in his dump-truck with a house built on its back, tried flying the balloon there, failed again and gave up. He decided to build a monument to God on a desert ridge instead. Carving and moulding the surface, using thousands of gallons of donated paint, he covered hundreds of metres of the ridge with evangelical messages and decorations. "God Is Love" flourished amidst fields of flowers and cascading waterfalls. After three years work the mountain collapsed, but instead of quitting, Knight learned from his mistakes, switched from using heavy concrete to lighter adobe to shape the mountain, and started over again. In 1994 local officials declared the mountain a toxic nightmare and tried to tear it down. Knight fought back, and with the help of friends and admirers disproved the government's claims. Today Salvation Mountain stands bigger than ever and Knight continues working on it, welcoming visitors by the hundreds from around the world.

Knight's evangelical message can be seen from far away as the mountain of adobe and paint just keeps growing.

Knights evangelische Botschaft auf dem künstlich errichteten und stetig wachsenden Berg ist weithin sichtbar.

Le message de paix lancé par Knight se voit de loin tandis que la montagne d'adobe peint ne cesse de grossir.

Leonard Knight (*1931) investierte fünf Jahre intensive Arbeit in einen Heißluftballon mit der Aufschrift »God Is Love«. Der Ballon war jedoch zu groß, als daß er hätte abheben können: Zum Schluß war er 100 Meter hoch. Im Jahr 1986 fuhr Knight ihn auf seinem Müllwagen mit aufgesetztem Haus in die Mojave-Wüste. Er versuchte, den Ballon endlich steigen zu lassen, scheiterte, gab seinen Plan auf und entschloß sich statt dessen, ein Gott gewidmetes Monument auf einem Höhenzug in der Wüste zu errichten. Er gestaltete die Felsoberfläche und brachte auf ihr mit Tausenden von Litern gespendeter Farbe Botschaften des Evangeliums und Verzierungen an. Der Berg erhielt den Namen »God Is Love« und wuchs in die Höhe, umgeben von Blumenfeldern und Wasserfällen. Nach drei Jahren fiel er in sich zusammen, aber Knight gab nicht auf, sondern lernte aus seinen Fehlern und errichtete einen neuen Berg, für den er nun Adobeziegel statt schweren Beton verwendete. Die örtlichen Behörden erklärten den Berg 1994 für verseucht und wollten ihn abreißen, aber Knight verteidigte ihn erfolgreich gemeinsam mit Freunden und Bewunderern. Heute erhebt sich Salvation Mountain höher denn je und zieht Hunderte von Besuchern aus der ganzen Welt an. Seine Arbeit setzt Knight natürlich fort.

Leonard Knight (*1931) tenta, avant d'édifier sa montagne du Salut, de fabriquer une gigantesque montgolfière portant l'inscription «Dieu est Amour». Vivant alors au Nebraska, il passa cinq ans à coudre un ballon qui finit par atteindre 100 mètres de hauteur et qu'il ne réussit pas à faire voler. Un beau jour, en 1986, il partit dans le désert Mojave, avec sa camionnette et sa petite maison posée dessus, dans l'espoir de réussir le lancement. Nouvel échec. C'est alors qu'il décide de construire un monument à la gloire de Dieu sur une crête du désert. Modelant la pente avec du ciment, sculptant, peignant à l'aide de milliers de litres de peinture qu'on lui offre, il recouvre des hectares de terrain avec des messages évangéliques et des motifs décoratifs. L'inscription «Dieu est Amour» s'étale au milieu des champs de fleurs et des cascades. Au bout de trois ans de travail, la montagne s'effondre. Knight reprend la tâche, remplaçant le ciment trop lourd par de l'adobe, plus léger. En 1994, les autorités locales décrètent que le site est hautement polluant et tentent de le détruire. Knight se bat et, avec l'appui d'amis et d'admirateurs, parvient à faire réviser la décision. Aujourd'hui, il travaille toujours à sa montagne du Salut, plus vaste que jamais, et accueille des centaines de visiteurs venus du monde entier.

Knight allows the paint to flow freely down the mountainside as he builds up his structure with bright colour and huge religious messages.

Die Farben fließen frei über den Hügelhang herab, der mit riesigen religiösen Botschaften in leuchtenden Farben verziert ist.

Knight laisse la peinture couler à son gré le long des pentes. Il mêle des motifs aux couleurs vives avec des inscriptions religieuses aux proportions gigantesques.

Knight's home is his trailer, richly decorated in his distinctive style and emblazoned with messages of love. Leonard Knight has lived without electricity for 17 years.

Knight wohnt in einem Wohnwagen, den er in seinem individuellen Stil und mit zahlreichen Friedensbotschaften dekoriert hat. Seit 17 Jahren lebt er ohne Elektrizität.

Knight vit dans sa maisonnette roulante, décorée de messages de paix et couverte de motifs qui caracté-risent son style si particulier. Il se passe d'électricité depuis 17 ans.

TheThunder MountainMon ument

Imlay, Nevada

Frank Van Zant (1921–1989), of Creek Indian descent, changed his name to **Rolling Mountain Thunder** after arriving in 1969 in the Thunder Mountain area of Nevada. Here he constructed three buildings of stone, cement and found materials, around which a framework supports over 200 painted cement figures and faces. The sculptures depict Native Americans and their protective spirits, as do a series of tableaux and murals. The framework rises above the main house forming a large handle so that, after death, the Great Spirit can carry it away. The site became a monument to the Native American and a refuge for outcasts and travellers, who stayed in Thunder's community without charge. Thunder saw it as a place embodying freedom and brotherhood for all. He suffered constant harassment from local people, and in 1983 the Visionary environment was partly destroyed by an arson attack, but it is still very impressive.

Die Vorfahren von Frank Van Zant (1921–1989) waren Creek-Indianer. Nach seinem Umzug 1969 in die Thunder Mountains von Nevada nahm er den Namen **Rolling Mountain Thunder** an und errichtete drei Gebäude aus Stein, Zement und Fundobjekten. Das umgebende Gerüst ist mit 200 farbigen Zementstatuen und -gesichtern geschmückt, die meist Indianer und ihre Schutzgeister darstellen. Wie ein überdimensionaler Henkel erhebt sich das Gerüst über dem Hauptgebäude, so daß der Große Geist es nach Thunders Tod leicht wegtragen kann. Reisende und Aussteiger fanden jederzeit eine Unterkunft auf dem Gelände, das zu einem indianischen Monument geworden war. Für Thunder war dieser Ort der Inbegriff von Freiheit und Brüderlichkeit. Der Künstler war ständig den Vorurteilen und Schikanen der örtlichen Bevölkerung ausgesetzt. So wurde das Visionary Environment 1983 durch einen Brandanschlag teilweise zerstört, aber es beeindruckt immer noch.

D'origine indienne creek, Frank Van Zant (1921–1989) prit le nom de **Rolling Mountain Thunder** («Tonnerre grondant de la montagne») lorsqu'il arriva en 1969 au Nevada, dans la région de Thunder Mountain. Là, il entreprit de construire trois édifices en pierre, en ciment et en matériaux de récupération. Le bâtiment principal était entouré d'une structure supportant plus de 200 personnages et visages en ciment peint; cet échafaudage formait une anse au-dessus de l'édifice, afin que le Grand Esprit puisse emporter ce dernier après la mort de son créateur. Sculptures, compositions et peintures représentaient des Indiens et des esprits protecteurs. Le site devint un monument dédié aux Indiens ainsi qu'un refuge gratuit pour les marginaux et les voyageurs. Pour son créateur, le lieu incarnait la liberté et la fraternité. Harcelé par la population locale, il vit son œuvre partiellement détruite en 1983, à la suite d'un incendie criminel, mais Thunder Mountain Monument est toujours très impressionnant.

The outside stairs lead to the deck where Thunder used to sit (left). The Pole of Humanity (facing page) depicts Native Americans, on whose suffering faces the years of deprivation are writ large.

Über die Außentreppe stieg Thunder hinauf zu der Plattform, wo er gerne saß (links). Die Gesichter der Indianer am Pfahl der Menschlichkeit (rechte Seite) sind erfüllt von dem Leid, das ihnen in vielen Jahren zugefügt wurde.

L'escalier extérieur (ci-contre) mène à la plate-forme où Rolling Mountain Thunder avait l'habitude de s'asseoir. Le mât de l'Humanité (page de droite) représente des Indiens dont le visage trahit les souffrances endurées pendant de longues années.

Several details from the Monument: the basket-like structure above the roof, a self-portrait of Thunder, holding a lightning bolt to strike down those who meant him harm (facing page, above right), a White man shooting a Native American, and the medicine man Tankan, standing watch (right).

Verschiedene Details: die korbähnliche Struktur auf dem Dach; ein Selbstporträt von Thunder, wie er mit dem Blitz in der Hand seine Feinde niederstreckt (linke Seite, oben rechts); ein Weißer, der einen Indianer erschießt; der wachestehende Medizinmann Tankan (rechts).

Détails du site: au-dessus du toit, la structure en forme d'anse; autoportrait de Thunder brandissant la foudre pour frapper ses ennemis (page de gauche, ci-dessus à droite); un homme blanc tirant sur un Indien; Tankan, homme médecine, faisant le guet (à droite).

197

The Totem PolePark

Foyil, Oklahoma

Nathan Edward Galloway (1880–1962) was a woodwork teacher, and after retirement in 1937, he started working on his monument to the Native American. The central feature is a 27-metre cement totem pole standing on a turtle's back and covered in reliefs of figures and faces, including representations of Sitting Bull and Geronimo. A smaller structure and a concrete tree are similarly embellished. Alongside them is the eleven-sided Fiddle House, originally Galloway's workshop and a display area for his wooden carvings and hand-made fiddles. After Galloway's death, the Totem Pole Park was abandoned, but in recent years it has been restored by volunteers from the Kansas Grassroots Art Association. The Park is now owned and operated by the Rogers County Historical Society.

Der Tischlermeister **Nathan Edward Galloway** (1880–1962) errichtete nach seiner Pensionierung ein Monument für die amerikanischen Ureinwohner, an dem er ab 1937 arbeitete. Das Hauptwerk bildet ein 27 Meter hoher Totempfahl aus Beton, der auf einer Schildkröte ruht und dessen Außenseite mit reliefierten Figuren und Gesichtern bedeckt ist, darunter Sitting Bull und Geronimo. Eine kleinere Ausgabe und ein Betonbaum wurden in derselben Weise gestaltet. Längs des Hauptgebäudes befindet sich das elfseitige Fiddle House, Galloways frühere Werkstatt und Ausstellungsraum für seine Schnitzereien und handgefertigten Geigen. Nach seinem Tod verfiel der Totem Pole Park zusehends und wurde erst vor wenigen Jahren von der Kansas Grassroots Art Association restauriert. Heute ist der Park im Besitz der Rogers County Historical Society.

Professeur de menuiserie, **Nathan Edward Galloway** (1880–1962) bâtit son monument aux Indiens après avoir pris sa retraite. L'élément central du site, réalisé à partir de 1937, est un totem de ciment de 27 mètres, perché sur le dos d'une tortue; il est décoré de personnages et de visages en bas-relief (tout comme un édifice plus petit et un arbre en béton), parmi lesquels on reconnaît Sitting Bull et Geronimo. Tout près se dresse la Fiddle House, ou Maison du violon, à onze côtés, qui servait d'atelier et de lieu d'exposition à Galloway pour ses sculptures sur bois et ses violons fabriqués à la main. Abandonné à la mort de son créateur, le site a été restauré ces dernières années par des bénévoles de la Kansas Grassroots Art Association. Aujourd'hui il appartient à la Rogers County Historical Society.

Ed Galloway's Totem Pole has four sculptures of Indians near the top, each representing a different tribe. It is covered in brightly painted motifs of Native America.

Auf der Spitze von Ed Galloways Totempfahl befinden sich die Skulpturen von vier Indianern, die verschiedene Stämme repräsentieren. Der Pfahl ist mit farbenfrohen indianischen Motiven dekoriert.

Les quatre personnages d'Indiens en haut du tipi-totem représentent chacun une tribu. L'ensemble est peint de motifs indiens aux couleurs vives.

TheWatts Towers

Los Angeles, California

Simon Rodia (1875–1965), ein italienischer Immigrant und Gelegenheitsarbeiter, arbeitete 33 Jahre an seinem außergewöhnlichen Bauwerk in Watts, einem Vorort von Los Angeles. Er begann 1921 den Bau, der aus drei hohen Türmen – der höchste ist 30 Meter hoch – und sechs niedrigeren besteht. Sie wurden alle aus Metallstangen und Rohren gefertigt, von denen er einige von Hand in die gewünschte Form brachte, indem er sie an den nahegelegenen Eisenbahnschienen verkeilte und dann umbog. Er verband die Stangen mit Drähten untereinander, stabilisierte sie mit Beton, während er die Außenflächen mit einem Mosaik aus Muscheln, Keramik- und Glasscherben auslegte. Eine Betonmauer, die mit Mosaiken, Reliefs und den Spuren von in den feuchten Zement gedrückten Werkzeugen verziert ist, umgibt die Anlage. Die Beweggründe für Rodias zwanghafte Kreativität sind nicht bekannt. Nach Fertigstellung seines Werkes vermachte er es einem Nachbarn und ging seiner Wege. Rodia entwarf keine Skizzen, verwendete weder Schrauben noch Schweißgeräte und arbeitete mit einem Minimum an finanziellen Mitteln. Die Watts Towers waren das erste amerikanische Environment, das internationale Anerkennung fand. Im Jahr 1958 forderte die Stadt Los Angeles wegen angeblich mangelnder Sicherheit den Abriß der Türme. Bei einer großen Protestdemonstration bewiesen Anhänger die Stabilität der Türme. Inzwischen hat die Stadt die Trägerschaft für die Türme übernommen und eine Million Dollar in die Renovierung investiert.

Simon Rodia (1875–1965), an Italian immigrant and itinerant worker, spent 33 years of his life on this extraordinary structure. Started in 1921, the three huge towers – the tallest is 30 metres high – and six shorter ones, were built of metal bars, pipes and rods, all bound together by wire. Rodia bent many of the metal parts by hand, wedging them under the rails of the nearby railway. The metal was then encased in concrete, and the surface decorated with a mosaic of broken crockery, glass and shells. Sited in the Los Angeles suburb of Watts, the Towers are surrounded by a concrete wall featuring patterned mosaics, relief elements and impressions of tools pressed into the wet cement. Rodia also built a series of small structures and seats at the foot of the Towers. Nobody knows what motivated Rodia's compulsive creativity; after the Towers were completed, he ceded them to a neighbour and went his way. He drew no plans, used neither bolts nor welds, and worked with minimum funding. The Watts Towers were the first American environment to gain international recognition. In 1958, the Los Angeles city authorities sought to demolish them, declaring them unsafe. Their safety was demonstrated by campaigning supporters, and the towers are now administered by the City, which has carried out a million-dollar restoration programme.

Immigré italien, travailleur itinérant avant d'entreprendre son œuvre, **Simon Rodia** (1875–1965) consacra 33 ans de sa vie à son extraordinaire construction. A partir de 1921, il commença à bâtir trois tours gigantesques, dont la plus haute culmine à trente mètres, et six de dimensions moindres, utilisant des barres en métal et des tuyauteries, liées avec des câbles et du fil de fer. Il courbait lui-même quantité d'éléments, en les coinçant d'abord sous les rails d'une voie ferrée toute proche. Une fois les structures assemblées, il noyait celles-ci dans le béton et les décorait de mosaïques en vaisselle cassée, en verre et en coquillages. Situées à Watts, banlieue de Los Angeles, les tours sont entourées d'un mur en béton orné de mosaïques, de bas-reliefs et de formes d'outils, imprimées en creux dans la surface encore humide. A la base des tours se trouvent des réalisations plus modestes et des sièges. N'utilisant ni soudure ni boulons, Rodia travailla sans plans et avec très peu de moyens. Personne ne sait ce qui le motiva tout au long de son entreprise. Lorsqu'il eut terminé, il céda l'ensemble à un voisin et poursuivit sa route. L'environnement fut le premier en Amérique à bénéficier d'une reconnaissance nationale. En 1958, les autorités de Los Angeles tentèrent de le faire démolir sous prétexte qu'il risquait de s'effondrer, mais une vigoureuse campagne de sauvegarde permit de prouver sa solidité. Le site est désormais géré par la municipalité qui a financé un programme de restauration d'un million de dollars.

The towers were constructed of metal rods and poles bent and wired together before being covered in cement. The outer wall of the Towers complex is richly adorned with mosaic and relief decoration. Old pots, broken bottles and ceramic fragments are embedded in the concrete.

Die Türme bestehen aus Metallstangen und Rohren, die gebogen, durch Kabel miteinander verbunden und mit Zement bedeckt wurden. Die Außenwände der Türme sind reich mit Reliefs und Mosaiken aus alten Töpfen, zerbrochenen Flaschen und Keramikscherben verziert.

Les tours sont construites avec des tiges et des barres de métal, courbées puis liées par des câbles et recouvertes de ciment. Le mur d'enceinte s'orne de quantité de mosaïques et de bas-reliefs; de vieux pots, des bouteilles cassées et des morceaux de céramiques sont incrustés dans le ciment.

Details showing the variety of found and broken objects used by Rodia to embellish his structure. Once under threat, the Watts Towers have now been listed as a National Monument.

Details zeigen die Bandbreite an Fundstücken und zerbrochenen Objekten, die Rodia für die Verschönerung seiner Türme verwendete. Einst waren sie vom Abriß bedroht, doch heute sind sie ein nationales Denkmal.

Ces détails de décoration montrent l'extraordinaire variété de matériaux et d'objets trouvés utilisés par Rodia pour embellir son œuvre. Autrefois menacées, les tours de Watts sont désormais classées monument national.

TheWind millPark

Lucama, North Carolina

When **Vollis Simpson** (*1919) retired in 1986 from his business of moving houses and barns and repairing mechanical equipment, he used some of the machine parts he had accumulated to build the first of over 30 huge whirligig sculptures. Having already harnessed windpower to provide his house with electricity and heating, he uses complex systems of cogs, gears and ball bearings to create beauty in motion. Figures, animals, and cut and painted sheet metal complete his colourful structures, which are covered with car reflectors to make them shine at night.

Vollis Simpson (*1919) zog sich 1986 aus Altersgründen aus seiner Elektrowerkstatt und Umzugsspedition zurück. Im Lauf seines Berufslebens hatte er zahllose Maschinenteile gesammelt, aus denen er das erste von insgesamt mehr als 30 überdimensionalen Mobiles gestaltete. Für die Versorgung mit Elektrizität und Warmwasser hatte Simpson bereits ein eigenes Windrad installiert, und nun bastelte er komplexe Konstruktionen aus Zahnrädern und Kugellagern, die sich elegant bewegten. Figuren, Tiere und Flugzeuge aus geschnittenem, buntem Blech ergänzen die farbenprächtigen Konstruktionen, die nachts effektvoll von Autoscheinwerfern und Reflektoren beleuchtet werden.

Vollis Simpson (*1919) possédait une entreprise qui déplaçait et remontait des bâtiments et réparait des machines. Il prit sa retraite en 1986 et, à partir de cette date, utilisa son stock de pièces mécaniques pour bâtir plus de 30 structures mues par le vent. Sachant maîtriser l'énergie éolienne qui fournissait déjà l'éclairage et le chauffage de sa maison, il créa des œuvres en mouvement grâce à un système compliqué d'engrenages et de roulements à billes. Ornées de personnages et d'animaux découpés dans la tôle et peints, ses structures colorées, couvertes de réflecteurs, brillent dans la nuit.

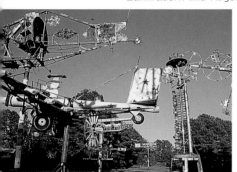

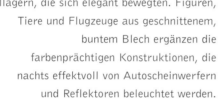

The visionary environment of Vollis Simpson includes some of the largest and most intricate whirligigs in America. The giant constructions tower above the ground as their complex gear mechanisms allow them to glide in movement. Some have hundreds of moving parts, and the surfaces of most of them are lined with car reflectors.

Das Visionary Environment von Vollis Simpson gehört zu den größten und interessantesten Mobile-Anlagen in den Vereinigten Staaten. Die riesigen Mobiles werden von komplexen Schaltmechanismen bewegt, so daß sie förmlich über der Erde zu schweben scheinen. Einige haben mehrere hundert bewegliche Teile, und an den meisten sind außerdem Autoscheinwerfer und Reflektoren angebracht.

L'environnement visionnaire de Vollis Simpson compte parmi les plus importants parcs à mobiles des Etats-Unis. Les gigantesques assemblages tournoyants se meuvent avec douceur grâce à des mécanismes sophistiqués. Quelques sculptures ont des centaines d'éléments en mouvement et la plupart sont recouvertes de réflecteurs et de rétroviseurs.

210

AsiaAsi enAsie &Africa AfrikaA frique

TheRockGarden ofChandigarh

Chandigarh, India

Nek Chand Saini (*1924), a humble transport official in the northern Indian city of Chandigarh, began in 1958 to clear a patch of jungle to make himself a small garden. He built a little hut, placed stones around the clearing, and sculpted a few figures from materials that lay to hand. Gradually his garden expanded; before long it covered several acres containing hundreds of sculptures set in a series of linked courtyards, even though building and development were forbidden in the area. Day after day, and at night by the light of burning tyres, he worked in total secrecy, in constant fear of being discovered. His materials were all reclaimed from the refuse tips of the city. He worked alone in this manner for 14 years, until discovered by a working party clearing the jungle. Amazed by what they had found, local government officials were thrown into turmoil. Nek Chand's creation was completely illegal – a development in a forbidden area – and should by rights have been demolished. There followed an enlightened decision: to give Nek Chand a salary to continue his work, and a small workforce. In 1976 the visionary environment was inaugurated as The Rock Garden of Chandigarh. Now comprising more than 25 acres of sculptures, buildings, arcades, gorges and waterfalls, it is acknowledged as one of the wonders of the modern world.

Nek Chand Saini (*1924), ein kleiner Beamter in der nordindischen Stadt Chandigarh, rodete 1958 im Dschungel ein Stück Land und legte einen kleinen Garten an. Trotz strengen Bebauungsverbotes errichtete er eine Hütte, grenzte die Lichtung mit Steinen ab und formte Skulpturen aus Materialien, die er von der städtischen Mülldeponie bezog. Allmählich wurde sein Garten immer weitläufiger und umfaßte mehrere miteinander verbundene Parzellen. Tag für Tag und Nacht für Nacht, beim Licht brennender Reifen, arbeitete Nek Chand unter völliger Geheimhaltung, immer mit der Angst, entdeckt zu werden. Nach 14 Jahren fand ein Dschungelrodungstrupp zufällig den Garten. Die örtlichen Behörden gerieten in große Verlegenheit, denn er war illegal und hätte vernichtet werden müssen. Trotzdem beschlossen sie, Nek Chand fortan ein Gehalt für die Fortsetzung seiner Arbeit zu zahlen. Chands phantastische Welt wurde 1976 als »The Rock Garden of Chandigarh« der Öffentlichkeit zugänglich gemacht. Heute umfaßt der Garten mehr als zehn Hektar Land mit Skulpturen, hohen Gebäuden, Arkaden, Schluchten und Wasserfällen und hat als eines der modernen Weltwunder Anerkennung gefunden.

Nek Chand Saini (*1924), modeste employé des transports publics de la ville de Chandigarh, au nord de l'Inde, commença son œuvre en 1958 en défrichant une parcelle de jungle pour y faire un petit jardin. Il bâtit une cabane, disposa des pierres autour du terrain et sculpta quelques personnages à partir des matériaux qu'il avait sous la main. Peu à peu, son entreprise prit de l'ampleur: il réalisa plusieurs centaines de sculptures qu'il disposa dans une suite d'espaces et de cours, occupant plusieurs hectares d'une zone pourtant déclarée inconstructible. Récupérant ses matériaux dans les décharges de la ville, s'éclairant la nuit avec des pneus qu'il faisait brûler, il travailla secrètement et en solitaire, craignant sans cesse d'être découvert. Ce qui advint au bout de 14 ans, la municipalité ayant décidé de nettoyer cet endroit envahi par la végétation. Stupéfaites, désemparées par l'illégalité du projet qui, normalement, aurait dû être démoli, les autorités finirent par prendre une décision courageuse: En 1976 elles accordèrent un salaire à Nek Chand pour qu'il puisse poursuivre sa tâche et lui fournirent une petite équipe. Le site devint officiellement le «Jardin de pierres de Chandigarh». Dix hectares où se mêlent des sculptures, de hauts bâtiments, des arcades, des cascades et des gorges, composent aujourd'hui ce que l'on considère comme l'une des merveilles du monde moderne.

212

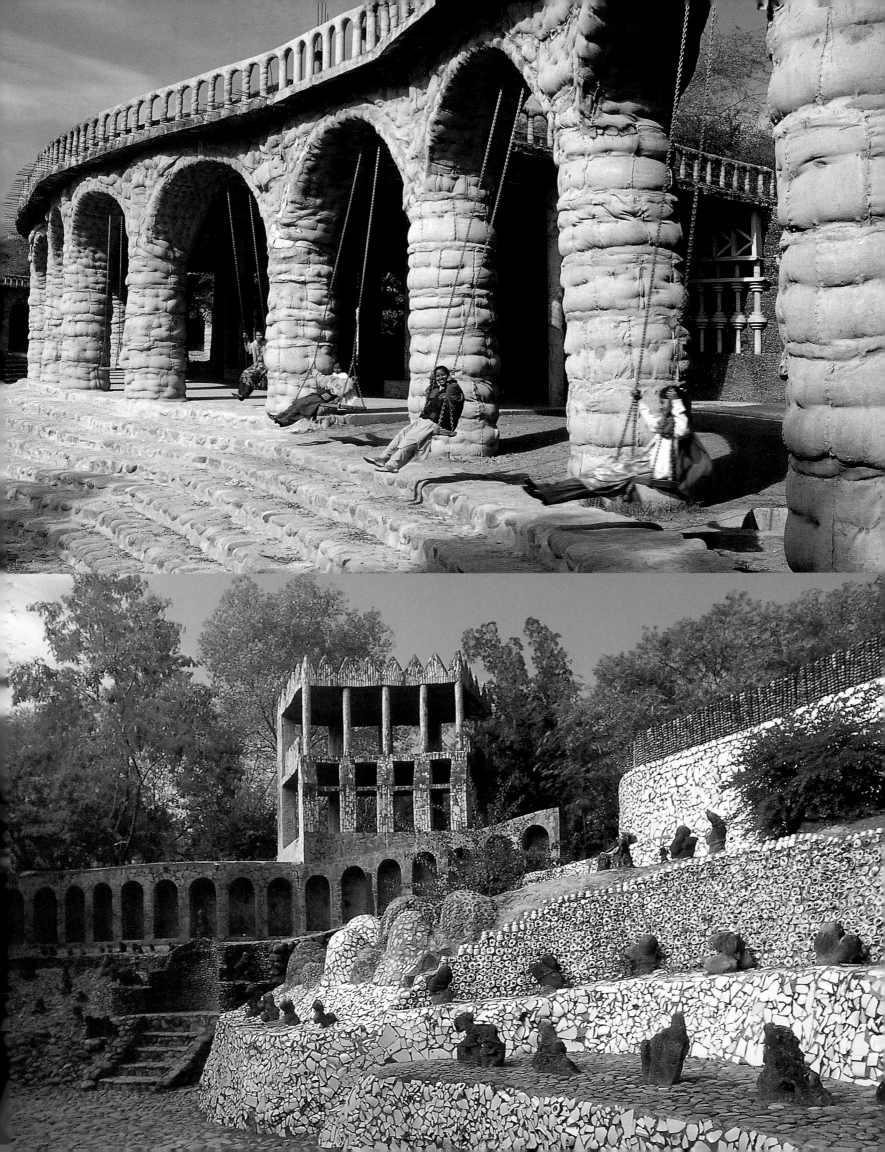

Countless figures of people and beasts inhabit Nek Chand's kingdom, all made of reclaimed materials. The ground they stand on is covered in a huge mosaic made from broken baths, basins and toilets. Huge family-sized swings hang beneath a sweeping columned walkway (previous page).

Nek Chands Königreich wird von zahllosen Statuen und Tierskulpturen aus Altmaterialien bewohnt. Das riesige Bodenmosaik setzt sich aus zerbrochenen Badewannen, Toiletten und Bidets zusammen. Große Schaukeln hängen von den Bögen einer von Säulen getragenen Arkade (vorhergehende Seite) herab.

D'innombrables sculptures, hommes ou bêtes, peuplent le royaume de Nek Chand. Fabriquées à partir de matériaux de récupération, elles se dressent sur un sol lui-même recouvert d'une immense mosaïque en morceaux de cuvettes, de baignoires et de sanitaires. Des arcades tout en courbes abritent de grandes balançoires (page précédente).

Flocks of birds stand along the top of the wall at the entrance to the rock garden, while every conceivable piece of broken crockery is used to clothe the cement figures.

Vogelschwärme krönen die Mauer am Eingang des Rock Garden. Jede verfügbare Keramikscherbe wurde zum Schmuck der Zementskulpturen verwendet.

Des vols d'oiseaux perchent sur le mur à l'entrée du Jardin de pierres. Les personnages sont habillés de débris de vaisselle cassée.

TheBuddhaPark Garden

Vientiane, Laos

Luangpu ("Venerable Grandfather") **Boonlour Sureerat**, the leader of his own religious sect, began working on Buddha Park Garden in 1958 to express his synthesis of Buddhist and Hindu teachings. Predominantly Buddhist in iconography, it also contains the figures of Shiva, Vishnu and other Hindu deities, alongside Chinese gods, characters from Thai mythology and secular and profane figures. The most imposing of these giant constructions is a globe 30 metres high. It has three floors, representing the three levels of existence: Hell, Earth, and Paradise. Visitors enter through the mouth of a dragon and climb a spiral staircase through a display of hundreds of small statues representing the inner and outer worlds of existence. The rooftop is a kind of belvedere with a panorama of the sculpture park. After the Communist takeover in 1977, Boonlour and his followers moved from Laos to neighbouring Thailand to create the Wat Khaek Buddha Park (see pages 220–221). The Laotian garden is now public property and a well-known tourist attraction.

Luangpu (»ehrwürdiger Großvater«) **Boonlour Sureerat**, Kopf und Gründer einer religiösen Sekte, gestaltete Buddha Park Garden ab 1958 als Ausdruck seiner persönlichen Lebenshaltung, die buddhistische und hinduistische Lehren verbindet. In der Anlage finden sich Shiva, Vishnu und andere hinduistische Gottheiten neben chinesischen Göttern, Figuren aus der thailändischen Mythologie und weltlichen Skulpturen. Das imposanteste der überdimensionalen Werke ist eine begehbare Weltkugel von 30 Metern Höhe. Die drei Stockwerke repräsentieren die drei Ebenen des Lebens: Hölle, Erde und Paradies. Durch ein Drachenmaul steigt man über eine Treppe hinauf zu einem Aussichtsturm, vorbei an zahllosen Statuen, die die inneren und äußeren Lebenswelten repräsentieren. Nachdem die Kommunisten 1977 in Laos die Macht ergriffen, wanderten Boonlour und seine Anhänger nach Thailand aus und errichteten dort den Wat Khaek Buddha Park (siehe Seite 220–221). Heute ist Buddha Park Garden Staatseigentum und eine beliebte Touristenattraktion.

Fondateur d'une secte religieuse, **Luangpu** («vénérable grand-père») **Boonlour Sureerat** commença en 1958 à construire le Buddha Park Garden pour donner corps à sa philosophie qui mêle étroitement les enseignements bouddhique et hindou. L'iconographie bouddhique prédomine mais le site abrite aussi des statues de Shiva, de Vishnou et d'autres divinités hindoues, de dieux chinois et de figures mythologiques thaïes, ainsi que de personnages profanes. Les édifices sont gigantesques; le plus imposant, un globe haut de 30 mètres, se divise en trois étages représentant les trois niveaux de l'existence: l'enfer, la terre et le paradis. On y pénètre par la gueule d'un dragon; un escalier en colimaçon, où sont exposées des centaines de statuettes évoquant la vie intérieure et la vie dans le monde, mène au sommet d'où l'on peut admirer le parc de sculptures. Après l'arrivée au pouvoir des communistes en 1977, Boonlour et ses fidèles ont quitté le Laos et ont entrepris de bâtir le Wat Khaek Buddha Park (voir pages 220–221), de l'autre côté de la frontière, en Thaïlande. Propriété de l'Etat, le parc est aujourd'hui très visité.

218

The Buddha Park Garden on the banks of the Mekong River contains more than 150 statues, reflecting Boonlour Sureerat's highly personal world view. Hindu, Buddhist and Chinese deities, characters from Thai mythology and secular sculptures are brought together in the park.

Der Buddha Park Garden am Ufer des Mekong umfaßt mehr als 150 Statuen, die Boonlour Sureerats ganz persönliche Lebenshaltung spiegeln. Unter ihnen befinden sich Hindu-Götter, buddhistische und chinesische Gottheiten, Figuren aus der Mythologie der Thai und weltliche Persönlichkeiten.

Situé sur les rives du Mékong, le Buddha Park Garden abrite plus de 150 statues, reflets de la vision du monde très personnelle de Boonlour Sureerat. Ici se mêlent des divinités hindoues, bouddhistes et chinoises, des héros de la mythologie thaïe et des personnages séculiers.

The Wat Khaek Buddha Park

Nong Khai, Thailand

After the communists took over, **Luangpu Boonlour Sureerat** left his native Laos and the Buddha Park Garden (see page 218–219) that he had created in Vientiane, bought 16 acres in neighbouring Thailand, and in 1977 set to work to recreate his first visionary environment on a larger scale. Like Boonlour's religious perspective, Wat Khaek combines Buddhist and Hindu elements, with huge statues of deities such as Shiva, Vishnu and Rama standing alongside mythological figures, representations of the Buddha, and images of Thai and Chinese gods. A Wheel of Life depicts the successive karmic stages. Secular tableaux include a group of dogs in human garb, illustrating the evils of drink, gambling and other vices. With over one hundred devotees to help him, Boonlour designs each figure, which is then constructed on metal supports and coated in unpainted concrete; larger structures have a brick interior. A huge temple, still under construction, its outer surface bristling with relief statuary, dominates the site. A museum-shrine contains framed pictures of deities and temple donors and of Boonlour at different stages of his life.

Nach der kommunistischen Machtübernahme verließ **Luangpu Boonlour Sureerat** Laos, kaufte 6,5 Hektar Land im Nordosten Thailands und gestaltete dort ab 1977 eine erweiterte Rekonstruktion seines ersten Werkes, des Buddha Park Garden in Vientiane (siehe Seite 218–219). Er ließ sich von buddhistischen und hinduistischen Lehren inspirieren und fertigte imposante und ausdrucksvolle Darstellungen von Shiva, Vishnu und Rama ebenso wie von Buddha, thailändischen und chinesischen Göttern, mythologischen Figuren und religiösen Ereignissen. Das Lebensrad repräsentiert den Ablauf des Lebens, während Hunde in Menschenkleidung Laster wie Trinkerei oder Glücksspiel versinnbildlichen. Gemeinsam mit seinen mehr als 100 begeisterten Anhängern konstruiert Boonlour Metallrahmen für die Skulpturen, mauert die großen Figuren innen aus und überzieht sie mit Zement. Beherrscht wird die Anlage von einem imposanten, noch im Bau befindlichen Tempel, dessen Außenwände zahlreiche Reliefs schmücken. In einem Gedenkschrein finden sich gerahmte Bilder von Göttern, Tempelgründern sowie von Boonlour selbst in verschiedenen Lebensaltern.

Après l'arrivée au pouvoir des communistes, **Luangpu Boonlour Sureerat** abandonne son Laos natal et le Buddha Park Garden (voir pages 218–219) qu'il y avait créé à Vientiane. Il s'installe au nord-est de la Thaïlande, pays voisin, et achète en 1977 6,5 hectares sur lesquels il entreprend de rebâtir son œuvre à plus grande échelle. A l'image de ses convictions religieuses, l'iconographie qu'il utilise évolue par rapport au premier site et combine avec plus de vigueur des thèmes bouddhiques et hindous. Il érige d'immenses statues de dieux tels que Shiva, Vishnou ou Rama, aux côtés de manifestations du Bouddha, de divinités thaïes et chinoises, de personnages mythologiques et de scènes sacrées. Une «Roue de l'existence» évoque les étapes de la naissance, de la vie et de la mort. Parmi les thèmes profanes, des chiens vêtus en hommes illustrent différents vices, comme l'alcool ou le jeu. Boonlour a de nombreux adeptes et bénéficie de l'aide d'une centaine de personnes. Il dessine les plans de chaque construction. Les statues se composent d'une armature en métal recouverte de béton nu, tandis que les structures plus importantes sont bâties sur de la brique. Toujours en cours de réalisation, un gigantesque temple croulant sous les bas-reliefs et les statues domine le site. Un sanctuaire-musée abrite des représentations de divinités ainsi que des photos de donateurs et de Boonlour lui-même, à différentes époques de sa vie.

TheWatTha wetLearn ingGarden

Sukhothai, Thailand

In 1975 the Buddhist monk **Phra Sumroeng** (1928–1995) was inspired by a dream of overwhelming intensity to build a garden in northern Thailand, containing over 100 life-size statues of painted concrete. In the tradition of temple "learning gardens", it vividly depicts the eternal punishments awaiting those who have sinned on Earth. Those who killed animals have the heads of their victims, those who abused alcohol have boiling liquids poured down their throats, those who struck or kicked others have huge hands and feet, while those who lied or used bad language have tiny mouths. The souls in torment are surrounded by tableaux depicting scenes from the life of Buddha and figures in devotional poses. Since Phra Sumroeng's death, work on the garden has continued under the guidance of Phra Banthoeng and the centrepiece, a large temple with intricate relief figures of Buddhist deities, is now nearing completion.

Ein Traum inspirierte den buddhistischen Mönch **Phra Sumroeng** (1928–1995) im Jahr 1975 dazu, mehr als 100 lebensgroße Statuen aus farbigem Zement zu errichten. Sie stehen in der Tradition der Tempellehrgärten und stellen anschaulich die Strafen dar, die irdische Sünder im Jenseits erwarten. Schlachter erhalten die Köpfe ihrer Opfer, Trinkern werden siedendheiße Flüssigkeiten eingeflößt, Gewalttäter haben überdimensionale Hände und Füße, Lügner und Lästerer erkennt man an dem winzigen Mund. Konventioneller sind dagegen die Darstellungen von Betenden und Szenen aus dem Leben Buddhas. Seit Phra Sumroengs Tod leitet Phra Banthoeng den Skulpturenpark im Norden Thailands und vollendet das Herzstück der Anlage, einen großen Tempel mit akkurat geschnitzten Reliefs von buddhistischen Gottheiten.

Le Wat Thawet Learning Garden au nord de la Thaïlande s'inscrit dans la tradition des jardins de méditation. A la suite d'un rêve en 1975, le moine bouddhiste **Phra Sumroeng** (1928–1995) a entrepris de créer plus de 100 statues grandeur nature, en béton peint, illustrant les châtiments infligés dans l'au-delà aux pécheurs d'ici-bas. Les hommes qui ont tué des animaux sont représentés avec les têtes de leurs victimes; les alcooliques sont forcés d'avaler des liquides bouillants; les violents ont des pieds et des mains d'une taille démesurée, qui signifie le mauvais usage qu'ils en ont fait, tandis que les menteurs et les grossiers sont figurés avec une toute petite bouche. Des scènes plus convenues montrent des épisodes de la vie de Bouddha ou des personnages dans des poses de dévotion. Depuis la mort de Phra Sumroeng, le travail continue sous la direction de Phra Banthoeng. L'élément central du site, un grand temple avec des bas-reliefs complexes de divinités bouddhistes, est presque achevé.

The statues in the Wat Thawet Learning Garden are arranged in exactly the order in which Phra Sumroeng saw them in his dream, so that visitors exploring the garden can share his dream experience. The final scene shows the faithful at prayer and sinners being punished in the Buddhist "Hell" (following pages).

Die Statuen im Wat Thawet Learning Garden sind genau so angeordnet, wie Phra Sumroeng sie in seinem Traum sah. Besucher können diese Traumerfahrung auch heute genau nachvollziehen. Die letzte Szene zeigt die Gläubigen beim Gebet und die Bestrafung der Sünder in der buddhistischen »Hölle« (folgende Doppelseite).

Les statues du jardin penché du Wat Thawet Learning Garden sont disposées suivant l'ordre exact dans lequel elles sont apparues en rêve à Phra Sumroeng, afin que les visiteurs partagent cette révélation. La dernière scène représente des fidèles en prière et des pécheurs subissant les châtiments de l'«enfer» bouddhiste (double page suivante).

The Aw Haw Gardens

Hong Kong

As a young man, **Aw Boon Haw** (1882–1954) was prevented from entering a park by a sign that read "No Entrance to dogs and Chinese". This experience marked him permanently. He went on to become the millionaire manufacturer of Tiger Balm, an all-purpose muscle analgesic sold throughout the Orient. His Tiger Balm garden in the Tai Hing district, dominated by the seven-storey Tiger Pagoda, was, from the outset, open to everyone, whatever their race. Built at a cost of 16 million Hong Kong dollars in 1935/1936, the seven-acre park is a more modest version of the Singapore garden. The array of brightly-painted kitsch sculptures was commissioned from local craftsmen. They depict figures from Chinese mythology and folk tales, major events in Chinese history, and Buddhist stories. There are strong moral overtones; the horrors that befall those who live a sinful life in this world are vividly depicted. The Ten Courts of Hell show the punishments meted out to unworthy sons, corrupt officials, unscrupulous traders, traitors, prostitutes, kidnappers, murderers, and rapists.

Als jungem Mann wurde **Aw Boon Haw** (1882–1954) das Betreten einer Parkanlage mit dem Hinweis »Zutritt für Hunde und Chinesen verboten« verwehrt. Diese Erfahrung belastete ihn ein Leben lang. Nachdem er durch die Herstellung von Tigerbalsam, einem Muskelanalgetikum, Millionär geworden war, errichtete er einen eigenen Garten, den von einer siebenstöckigen Tigerpagode dominierten Tiger Balm Garden im Distrikt Tai Hing. Der drei Hektar große Park, eine bescheidenere Ausgabe der Haw Par Villa in Singapur, wurde 1935/1936 errichtet und stand den Menschen aller Rassen offen. Aw Boon Haw investierte 16 Millionen HK-Dollar und beschäftigte zahllose Facharbeiter mit der Gestaltung farbenprächtiger Skulpturen, die Figuren der chinesischen Mythologie, aus Volksmärchen, bedeutenden Ereignissen der chinesischen Geschichte sowie buddhistischen Sagen darstellen. Ein wichtiges Thema in diesem Garten sind die Strafen, die irdische Sünder im Jenseits erwarten: Die zehn Höfe der Hölle veranschaulichen die Strafen für Mörder, korrupte Beamte, Verräter, Prostituierte, Vergewaltiger und skrupellose Geschäftsleute.

Jeune homme, **Aw Boon Haw** (1882–1954) se heurta devant un parc à un panneau qui en interdisait l'entrée «aux chiens et aux Chinois». Il n'oublia jamais cette mésaventure. Devenu millionnaire grâce à son baume du tigre – un analgésique vendu dans toute l'Asie et destiné à guérir d'innombrables maux, il entreprit de créer un univers merveilleux ouvert à tous, sans distinction de race. A l'ombre de la pagode du Tigre, haute de sept étages, dans le district de Tai Hing, le parc de trois hectares fut construit en 1935/1936; Aw Boon Haw y investit 16 millions de dollars de Hong-kong. Il s'agit d'une version réduite du parc qu'il créa à Singapour. Des artisans locaux réalisèrent les sculptures kitsch aux couleurs vives qui représentent des personnages mythiques chinois, des contes populaires, de grands événements de l'histoire chinoise et des épisodes de la tradition bouddhique. L'ensemble est très moralisateur et montre les malheurs qui s'abattent dans l'au-delà sur les pécheurs. Les scènes des Dix Tribunaux de l'Enfer détaillent les châtiments infligés aux fils indignes, aux ravisseurs, aux assassins, aux fonctionnaires corrompus, aux traîtres, aux prostituées, aux violeurs et aux commerçants véreux.

TheHaw ParVilla

Singapore

The greater of the two gardens commissioned by **Aw Boon Haw** (1882–1954) in the Thirties, Haw Par Villa is a Chinese mythological theme park featuring the gaudy figurative displays that are an Aw Boon Haw trademark. The tableaux depict scenes from Chinese mythology and the moral lessons to be learned from pleasure and its punishment. The Ten Courts of Hell show sinners in the afterlife, suffering horribly for their misdemeanours on Earth. The sins of indulgence, gambling, drunkenness and debauchery are shown to incur terrible retribution. Opened in March 1937, the park and the villa were ransacked during the Second World War by Japanese troops, who murdered Aw Boon Haw's brother and stole priceless family collections. Since then it has been fully restored and new additions are still being made to this landmark of Oriental kitsch.

Haw Par Villa ist der größere von zwei Gärten, die in den dreißiger Jahren von **Aw Boon Haw** (1882–1954) angelegt wurden. Der mythologische Themenpark bietet farbenprächtige Skulpturengruppen, das Markenzeichen von Aw Boon Haw. Szenen aus der chinesischen Mythologie versinnbildlichen moralische Lehren, während in den zehn Hallen der Hölle Sünder im Jenseits und die schrecklichen Strafen für ihre Laster dargestellt werden, zum Beispiel Völlerei, Glücksspiel, Trinkerei und andere Ausschweifungen. Villa und Park wurden im März 1937 geöffnet, aber im Zweiten Weltkrieg von japanischen Truppen geplündert. Aw Boon Haws Bruder wurde getötet und die unschätzbaren Familienerbstücke gestohlen. Heute ist dieses Wahrzeichen orientalischen Kitsches vollständig restauriert und wird ständig erweitert.

Haw Par Villa, le plus grand des deux parcs que **Aw Boon Haw** (1882–1954) fit construire dans les années trente, est un jardin thématique consacré à la mythologie chinoise. Sculptures et édifices tape-à-l'œil, caractéristiques des réalisations de l'homme d'affaires, se mêlent à des scènes mythologiques ou moralisantes, illustrant les leçons qu'il faut tirer des plaisirs et des châtiments. Les «Dix Tribunaux de l'Enfer» décrivent les supplices endurés après leur mort par ceux qui ont péché ici-bas. Des souffrances terribles punissent ainsi la faiblesse, le jeu, l'ivrognerie et la débauche. Pendant la Seconde Guerre mondiale, les troupes japonaises saccagèrent le parc et la villa inaugurés en mars 1937, tuèrent le frère de Aw Boon Haw et volèrent des collections inestimables appartenant à la famille. Depuis, le site a été entièrement restauré et de nouveaux aménagements sont en cours dans ce haut lieu du kitsch oriental.

The 60-metre-long Dragon, the largest in South East Asia, guards the entrance to Haw Par Villa (above). One of the tableaux shows the three San Gau sisters confronting Jiang Zi Ya at the Battle of the Yellow River (facing page).

Der 60 Meter lange Drache, einer der größten in Südostasien, bewacht den Eingang der Haw Par Villa (oben). Eines der Tableaux zeigt die drei San-Gau-Schwestern, die Jiang Zi Ya in der Schlacht am Gelben Fluß bekämpfen (rechte Seite).

Un dragon minéral long de 60 mètres, le plus grand d'Asie du Sud-Est, garde l'entrée de la villa (ci-dessus). Une des scènes montre les trois sœurs San Gau affrontant Jiang Zi Ya, au cours de la bataille du Fleuve Jaune (page de droite).

Further tableaux show the Chinese hero Xue Ren Gui reconquering the Western territories of China, which were constantly under rebel and barbarian attack (facing page above), the Red Lotus temple being cleared of evil monks (facing page below), Hua Guo Shan, the Mountain of Flowers and Fruits, which is the birthplace of the Monkey god (right and below), the moral tales of Thrift Not Theft according to which being thrifty is an important step on the path to virtue, and the story of the Grateful Tortoise, a popular tale of good deeds receiving due reward.

Weitere Tableaux zeigen den chinesischen Helden Xue Ren Gui bei der Eroberung Westchinas, das immer wieder von Rebellen und Invasoren angegriffen worden war (linke Seite oben), die Bestrafung unsittlicher Mönche aus dem Roten Lotostempel (linke Seite unten), den Berg der Blüten und Früchte Hua Guo Shan, der auch der Geburtsort des Affengottes ist (rechts und unten), moralisierende Erzählungen, die Diebstahl anprangern und Sparsamkeit als eine wichtige Tugend feiern sowie die populäre Geschichte der dankbaren Schildkröte, in der gute Taten belohnt werden.

Le héros chinois Xue Ren Gui combat pour conquérir les régions occidentales de la Chine, en rébellion constante et menacées par les attaques barbares (page de gauche, en haut). Les moines débauchés sont chassés du temple du Lotus Rouge (page de gauche, en bas). Hua Guo Shan, la montagne des Fleurs et des Fruits où naquit le dieu Singe (à droite et ci-dessous), des contes moralisateurs selon lesquels le vol est un vice et l'économie une étape importante sur le chemin de la vertu et la légende de la tortue reconnaissante, mythe populaire qui voit les bonnes actions récompensées.

Aeroplane

Bergville, South Africa

As a young schoolboy, **Punch Mbhele** (*1969) followed the African tradition and built his own toys. However, in 1986 he moved on from wire-frame cars to making aeroplanes out of scrap metal. Soon his creations were in evidence throughout the area of Natal where he lived. Usually stuck high on poles, his aeroplanes were enthusiastically received by local people, who supported Mbhele by buying and displaying his work. His most ambitious project was his house. Made from a framework of old telegraph poles and scrap wood, with a skin of old van parts, it was planned as an aeroplane, then became a helicopter, and ended up as a fish.

Tout jeune, encore écolier, **Punch Mbhele** (*1969) reprend la tradition africaine des jouets fabriqués à la maison. Il confectionne d'abord des voitures avec une armature en fil de fer, avant de créer des avions en ferraille à partir de 1986. Bien vite, il dissémine ses créations autour de chez lui, dans la province de Natal, accrochant ses zincs à de grands poteaux. Les voisins accueillirent son initiative avec enthousiasme et l'encouragèrent en achetant et en exposant ses œuvres. Mbhele entreprit ensuite de bâtir sa maison dans la même veine: il construisit une armature de vieux poteaux télégraphiques et de pieux en bois, qu'il recouvrit de pièces prises sur de vieux camions. D'abord conçue comme un avion, l'habitation s'est transformée en hélicoptère avant de devenir poisson.

Als Schuljunge bastelte **Punch Mbhele** (*1969) – wie die meisten afrikanischen Kinder – sein Spielzeug selbst. Ab 1986 wechselte er von Drahtautos zu Altmetallflugzeugen, die er auf hohen Pfählen rings um seine Wohnung in der Provinz Natal aufstellte. Seine Nachbarn waren begeistert und unterstützten ihn, indem sie seine Arbeiten kauften und ausstellten. Sein anspruchsvollstes Projekt war die Gestaltung seines Hauses, eine Konstruktion aus alten Telegrafenmasten, Altholz und ausgedienten Autoteilen. Ursprünglich sollte es ein Flugzeug darstellen, wurde dann aber zu einem Hubschrauber umgestaltet und schließlich als Fisch vollendet.

Mbhele's creations can be seen throughout his valley. In his aeroplane-fish home, built in the middle of his village, he has a telephone and TV. Below: the workshop and sitting room.

Mbheles Werk liegt im Zentrum des Dorfes und ist schon von weitem sichtbar. Das Haus in Form eines "Flugzeugfisches" verfügt über Telefon und Fernseher. Unten: Atelier und Wohnzimmer.

Les œuvres de Mbhele sont visibles partout dans la vallée. Au milieu du village se dresse sa maison, mi-poisson, mi-avion, avec téléphone et télévision. En bas: l'atelier et le salon.

TheOwl House

Nieu Bethesda, South Africa

Beginning in 1955, **Helen Martins** (1898–1976) created a haven of light within her home in the Cape Province, replacing walls with huge windows and covering surfaces with coloured ground glass. She positioned shaped mirrors to reflect the sun, moon and stars at dawn and dusk. Hundreds of candles and coloured paraffin lights completed the effect and gave the interior an overpowering warmth. The house is surrounded by 65 cement owls and a procession of camels facing the East, accompanied by wise men, worshippers and pilgrims. This she named the Camel Yard, and covered it with netting, creating an aviary so that birds could fly among the 300 or more statues. She was helped in her project by three African labourers, especially by Koos Malgas, who built most of the cement sculptures under her direction. Old beer and wine bottles feature in the sculpted figures and are used in the construction of several buildings symbolising Mecca, a place that haunted Martin's imagination. Ostracised by her strict Calvinist community, she lived an isolated existence in her self-made world, eventually committing suicide by drinking caustic soda. Her story was immortalised by South African playwright Athol Fugard in his work "The Road to Mecca".

Helen Martins (1898–1976) schuf in ihrem »Eulenhaus« ab 1955 eine Oase des Lichts: Sie ersetzte die Wände ihres Hauses in der Kapprovinz durch Fenster, legte die Oberflächen mit farbigem Mattglas aus und plazierte Spiegel in den verschiedensten Formen, die das Licht von Sonne, Mond und Sternen während der Dämmerung reflektieren. Hunderte von Kerzen und Öllampen schenken dem Haus ein überwältigend warmes Licht. Rundum stehen 65 Zementeulen, während Vögel in dem von einem Netz abgedeckten »Kamelgehege« umherfliegen, wo eine Karawane von mehr als 300 Skulpturen – Kamele, Weise und Pilger – nach Osten zieht. Unterstützt wurde Helen Martins von drei Afrikanern, insbesondere von Koos Malgas, der unter ihrer Anleitung die meisten der Zementskulpturen herstellte. Sie verwendeten auch Bier- und Weinflaschen für die Figuren und die Darstellungen von Mekka – ein Ort, der Helen Martins zeitlebens faszinierte. Sie wurde von der streng kalvinistischen Gemeinde ausgestoßen und lebte völlig isoliert in ihrer eigenen Welt, bis sie sich 1976 mit Ätznatron das Leben nahm. In seinem Werk »Der Weg nach Mekka« erzählt der südafrikanische Dramatiker Athol Fugard ihre Lebensgeschichte.

Labourer at the entrance of the Owl House (above).
Ein Arbeiter am Eingang des Owl House (oben).
Un travailleur à l'entrée de la Owl House (ci-dessus).

Helen Martins (1898–1976) fit de sa maison du Cap à partir de 1955 un paradis de lumière, remplaçant les murs par d'immenses baies vitrées et recouvrant les parois restantes de verre pilé de couleur. Elle disposa des miroirs aux formes variées de telle sorte qu'ils réfléchissent le soleil, la lune et les étoiles à l'aube et au crépuscule. Des centaines de bougies et de lumignons de couleur à la paraffine rendaient l'ensemble merveilleusement chaleureux. Autour de sa maison se dressent 65 hiboux en ciment et une procession de chameaux tournés vers l'est, accompagnés de sages, de fidèles et de pèlerins. Helen Martins recouvrit d'un treillage la «Cour des chameaux», comme elle l'appelait, et y enferma des oiseaux, la transformant en une volière aux 300 statues. Elle travailla avec l'aide de trois ouvriers africains, et en particulier avec Koos Malgas qui réalisa sous sa direction la plupart des sculptures en ciment. Eléments utilisés dans les statues, de vieilles bouteilles de vin et de bière composent également plusieurs édifices symbolisant La Mecque, lieu qui obsédait Helen Martins. Tenue à l'écart par le milieu calviniste très strict où elle était née, elle mena une existence solitaire dans l'univers qu'elle avait créé. Elle finit par se suicider en avalant de la soude caustique. Le dramaturge sud-africain Athol Fugard a retracé son destin dans une pièce intitulée «The Road to Mecca».

Details: a view through the Camel Yard's arch toward the kitchen (facing page); a languid mermaid floats over the kitchen window; a praying figure faces the sun; the Mona Lisa is one of the dominating motifs of The Owl House; worshippers facing East; an archway swathed in owls and camels (below right).

Verschiedene Details: Blick durch das Kamelgehege zur Küche (linke Seite), über deren Fenster sich eine schmachtende Seejungfrau räkelt; ein Sonnenanbeter; die Mona Lisa ist eines der vorherrschenden Motive des Owl House; Eulen und Kamele zieren einen Bogen (unten rechts).

Détails du site: l'arcade de la Cour des chameaux et, au fond, la cuisine (page de gauche); au-dessus de la fenêtre flotte une sirène langoureuse; un personnage en prière, face au soleil; la Joconde, un thème récurrent de la Owl House; des fidèles tournés vers l'orient; un arc peuplé de hiboux et de chameaux (ci-dessous à droite).

A camel silently watches a relief with a white stork flying over the sun (left). Mermaids beck
one to explore further (below left). Koos Malgas portrayed his daughters in the sculptures
two young girls (below right). Two young men struggle in vain to hold back the inevitable po
sage of time as it ticks by on the church steeple (facing page).

Ein Kamel blickt auf die reliefierte Darstellung eines weißen Storches, der über die Sonne flie
(links). Seejungfrauen laden zum weiteren Entdecken ein (unten links). Koos Malgas porträti
te in den Skulpturen zweier junger Mädchen seine Töchter (unten rechts). Zwei junge Männ
kämpfen vergeblich gegen den unaufhaltsamen Lauf der Zeit, die durch den Kirchturm sy
bolisiert wird (rechte Seite).

Un chameau tourne la tête vers un relief qui représente une cigogne survolant le soleil (à ga
che). Des sirènes invitent le visiteur à s'avancer (ci-dessous à gauche). Koos Malgas a rep
senté ici ses deux filles (ci-dessous à droite). Deux jeunes hommes s'efforcent en vain d'arrê
le temps qui passe au cadran du clocher (page de droite).

1. BOOKS

Arz, Claude: Guide de la France Insolite, Hachette, Paris 1990

Arz, Claude: La France Insolite, Hachette, Paris 1995

Aulakh, Malkiat Singh: The Rock Garden, Tagore Publishers, Ludhiana 1986

Beardsley, John, and Pierce, John (Photographer): Gardens of Revelation: Environments by Visionary Artists, Abbeville Press, New York 1994

Bihalji-Merin, Oto: Modern Primitives, Thames & Hudson, London 1971

Bihalji-Merin, Oto, and Nebojsa-Bato, Tomasevic: World Encyclopedia of Naive Art, Frederick Muller, London 1984

Borg, Jorgen, and Cronhammar, Ingvar: Gars du Nord, Maison du Danemark, Paris 1988

Bouchart, François-Xavier, and Beauthéac, Nadine: Jardins fantastiques, Editions du Moniteur 1982

Blasdel, Gregg, and Lipke, William C: Clarence Schmidt, Fleming Museum, University of Vermont, Burlington

Brackman, Barbara, Dwigans, Cathy (Editors) et al.: Backyard Visionaries: Grassroots Art in the Midwest, University Press of Kansas, Lawrence 1998

Brousse, Robert, et al: Masgot, Lucien Souny, France 1993

Burgess, Karen E., and Owen Jones, Michael (Editor): Home Is Where the Dog Is: Art in the Back Yard (Folk Art and Artists Series), University Press of Mississippi, Jackson 1996

Catalogue des travaux de Jean Dubuffet: Habitats, Closerie Falballa, Salon d'été, Paris 1981

Cardinal, Roger: Outsider Art, Studio Vista, London and Praeger, New York 1972.

Chazaud, Pierre: Du Facteur Cheval à l'art moderne, Editions du Mandala, Toulaud 1991 (English version: From the Facteur Cheval to Modern Art, Editions du Mandala, Toulaud 1991)

Christy, Jim: Strange Sites: Uncommon Homes and Gardens of the Pacific Northwest, Harbour Publishing, Canada 1996

Clarke, Ethne, and Wright, George: English Topiary Gardens, Weidenfeld and Nicolson, London 1988 (reprinted 1997)

Collins, George, Elffers, Joost, and Schuyt, Michael: Fantastic Architecture, New York 1980 (German version: Phantastische Architektur, DuMont Buchverlag, Cologne 1980; French version: Les Bâtisseurs de Rêve, Hachette, Paris 1980)

Danchin, Laurent: Chomo, Simoën, Paris 1978

Danchin, Laurent: Le Manège de Petit Pierre, La Fabuloserie, Dicy 1995

Danchin, Laurent: Jean Dubuffet, La Manufacture, Paris 1988

David, Francis: Guide de L'Art Insolite, Nord – Pas-de-Calais, Herscher, Paris 1984

Dinsmoor, Samuel Perry: Pictorial History of The Cabin Home in Garden of Eden, Lucas, Kansas, n.d.

Ditzen, Lore: Nek Chand, Haus der Kulturen der Welt, Berlin 1992

Dubuffet, Jean: Prospectus et tous écrits suivants, 4 vols, Gallimard, Paris 1967

Dubuffet, Jean: Asphyxiante culture, Jean-Jacques Pauvert, Paris 1968 (English version: Asphyxiating Culture and Other Writings, Four Walls Eight Windows, New York 1988; German version: Schriften, 4 Bde Gachnang und Springer 1991–1994)

Ehrmann, Gilles: Les Inspirés et leurs demeures, Editions du Temps, Paris 1961

Fenoli, Marc: Le Palais idéal du Facteur Cheval, Editions Glénat, Grenoble 1990

Finster, Howard et al.: Howard Finster: Man of Visions Now on this Earth, Abbeville Press New York 1989

Fuks, Paul: Picassiette, Le Jardin d'Assiettes, Ides et Calendes, Neuchâtel 1992

Garcet, Robert: Eben-Ezer en Er Was Eens, Drukkerij Rosbeek Nuth, Holland 1997

Goekjian, Karekin, Peacock, Robert, and Wertkin, Gerard C.; Light of the Spirit: Portraits of Southern Outsider Artists, University Press of Mississippi, Jackson 1998

Goldstone, Bud, and Paquin Goldstone, Arloa: The Los Angeles Watts Towers, Thames and Hudson, London 1997; JP Getty Foundation 1997

Graatsma, William Pars: Eben Ezer, Graatsma, Maastricht 1996

Green, Candida Lycett, and Lawson, Andrew: Brilliant Gardens: A Celebration of English Gardening, Chatto & Windus, London 1989

Granö, Veli: Onnela, Lahti, Finland 1989

Hall, Michael D., Cardinal, Roger, and Metcalf, Eugene W. (Editors): The Artist Outsider, Creativity and the Boundaries of Culture, Smithsonian Institute Press 1994

Headley, Gwyn, and Meulenkamp, Wim: Follies, Jonathan Cape, London 1986

Hemphill, Herbert Waide Jr, and Weissman, Julia: Twentieth Century Folk Art and Artists, JP Dutton, New York 1974

Isaacs, Jennifer: Quirky Gardens, Ten Speed Press, Berkeley 1995

Jakovsky, Anatole: Dämonen und Wunder, DuMont Buchverlag, Cologne 1963

Jones, Barbara Mildred: Follies and Grottoes, Constable, London 1953 (reprinted 1974)

Jounnais, Jean-Yves: Des Nains, Des Jardins, Hazan, Paris 1993

Kemp, Kathy, and Boyer, Keith (Photographer): Revelations: Alabama's Visionary Folk Artists, Crane Hill, Birmingham, Alabama 1994

Kirby, Doug, Smith, Ken, and Wilkins, Mike: The New Roadside America, Simon & Schuster, New York 1986 (revised edition Fireside 1992)

Kloos, Marten: Le Paradis terrestre de Picassiette, Encre, Paris 1979

Koller, Karl Heinz: Hundertwasserhaus, Verlag Georg Prachner, Vienna 1990 (reprinted Museum Betriebs GmbH 1997)

Lambton, Lucinda: An Album of Curious Houses, Chatto & Windus, London 1988

Lanoux, Jean-Louis: Chomo l'été, Chomo l'hiver, Fondation Chomo, Paris 1987

Lassus, Bernard: Jardins Imaginaires: Les habitants-paysagistes, Seuil, Paris 1977

Lewery, Anthony J.: Popular Art: Past and Present, David & Charles, Newton Abbot 1991

Lycett Green, Candida, and Lawson, Andrew: Brilliant Gardens, Chatto & Windus, London 1989

MacGregor, John M.: The Discovery of the Art of the Insane, Princeton University Press, Princeton 1989

Maizels, John: Raw Creation: Outsider Art and Beyond, Phaidon Press, London 1996

Manley, Roger: Signs and Wonders: Outsider Art Inside North Carolina, North Carolina Museum of Art, Raleigh 1989

Manley, Roger, and Sloan, Mark: Self-Made Worlds: Visionary Folk Art Environments, Aperture New York 1997

Margolis, John: Fun Along the Road, Bullfinch, Boston New York 1998

Metz, Holly: Two Arks, A Palace, Some Robots & Mr Freedom's Fabulous Fifty Acres, City Without Walls, Newark, New Jersey 1989

Mihailescu, Anca, and Pestarque, Gerard: Sapinta, The Merry Cemetery, Editions Hesse, Paris 1991

Mookerjee, Priya: Pathway Icons: The Wayside Art of India, Thames & Hudson, London 1987

Moses, Kathy: Outsider Art of the South, Schiffer Arglen PA 1999

Mutoo, Henry D., and Craig, Karl "Jerry": My Markings, The Art of Gladwyn K. Bush, Cayman National Cultural Foundation, Grand Cayman, British West Indies 1994

Navratil, Leo: August Walla, Greno, Vienna 1988

Niles, Susan A.: The Dickeyville Grotto: The Vision of Father Matthias Wernerus, University Press of Mississippi, Jackson 1997

Owen, Jane: Eccentric Gardens, Pavilion, London 1990

Patterson, Tom: St. EOM in the Land of Pasaquan, The Jargon Society, Winston-Salem 1987

Peacock, Robert, and Jenkins, Annibel: Paradise Garden: A Trip through Howard Finster's Visionary World, Chronicle, San Francisco 1996

Prévost, Claude and Clovis, and Jouve, Pierre Jean: Le Palais idéal du Facteur Cheval, (revised edition), ARIE, Hédouville 1994

Prévost, Claude and Clovis: Les Bâtisseurs de L'Imaginaire, Editions de l'Est, Jarville-la-Malgrange 1990

Prinzhorn, Hans et al.: Bildnerei der Geisteskranken, Verlag Julius Springer, Heidelberg 1922 (reprinted 1997; English version: Artistry of the Mentally Ill, Springer-Verlag New York 1972, reprinted 1995)

Purser, Philip: Where Is He Now? The Extraordinary World of Edward James, Quartet, London 1978

Rosen, Seymour: In Celebration of Ourselves, California Living Books, San Francisco 1979

Rosen, Seymour, and LaPorte, Paul: Simon Rodia's Towers in Watts, LACMA, Los Angeles 1962

Rosenak, Chuck and Jan: Encyclopedia of Twentieth-Century American Folk Art and Artists, Abbeville Press, New York 1990

Rosenak, Chuck and Jan: Contemporary American Folk Art: A Collector's Guide, Abbeville Press, New York 1996

Rufus, Anneli S., and Lawson, Kristan: Europe Off The Wall: A Guide to Unusual Sights, John Wiley & Sons, New York 1988

Rufus, Anneli S., and Lawson, Kristan: Weird Europe: A Guide to Bizarre, Macabre and Just Plain Weird Sights, Griffin Trade Paperback 1999

Ryczko, Joe: Les excentriques du pays aux bois, Editions Plein Chant 1991

Saint Phalle, Niki de et al.: Niki de Saint Phalle: The Tarot Garden, Charta 1998

Schubert, Marcus: Outsider Art II Visionary Environments, Art Random, Kyoto Shoin 1991

Sellen, Betty-Carol, Johanson, Cynthia: 20th Century American Folk, Self Taught and Outsider Art, Neal-Schuman, New York 1993

Stone, Lisa, and Zanzi, Jim: Sacred Spaces and Other Places: A Guide to Grottos and Sculptural Environments in the Upper Midwest, The School of the Art Institute of Chicago Press 1993

Stone, Lisa, and Zanzi, Jim: The Art of Fred Smith, Weber & Sons, Park Falls, Winsconsin 1991

Angelika Taschen (Editor): Hundertwasser Architektur, Benedikt Taschen Verlag, Cologne 1996 (also English and French version)

Tatin, Robert: Etrange Musée – Robert Tatin, Librairie Charpentier, Paris 1977

Thévoz, Michel: Art Brut, Skira, Geneva, 1975 (English version: Skira, London and New York, 1976, reprinted 1995)

Thiébaut, Olivier: Bonjour aux promeneurs! Editions Alternatives, Paris 1996

Verroust, Jacques, and Lacarrière, Jacques (text): Les Inspirés du Bord des Routes, Les Presses de la Connaissance, Paris 1978

Vertikoff, Alexander (Photographer), Sharpe, Mal and Sandra: Weird Rooms, Pomegranate, San Francisco 1996

Vogel, Susan (Editor): Africa Explores: 20th Century African Art, Center for African Art, New York 1991 (reprinted Prestel Verlag, Munich New York 1994)

Wampler, Jan: All Their Own: People and the Places They Build, Schenkman Publishing Company, Cambridge, Massachusetts 1977

Younge, Gavin: Art of the South African Townships, Thames and Hudson, London 1988

Weiner Longhauser, Elsa, Szeemann, Harald, and Wertkind, Gerard C.: Self Taught Artists of the 20th Century: An American Anthology, Chronicle Books, San Francisco 1998

Yust, Larry, and Knight, Leonard: Salvation Mountain, New Leaf Press, Los Angeles 1998

2. COLLECTIVE WORKS

Chomo, Societe Litteraire des P.T.T., Paris 1991

Niki de Saint Phalle, Nassau County Museum of Fine Art, New York 1988

Environments by Self-Taught Artists, Public Art Review, Issue 7 Volume 4, Milwaukee Summer/Fall 1992

Grassroots Art in Twelve New Jersey Communities, Kansas Grassroots Art Association, Lawrence 1989

Home Is What You Make It, Horizon, 1964

Naives and Visionaries, Walker Art Center, EP Dutton, New York 1974

Outsiders, Arts Council of Great Britain, London 1979

Les Singuliers de l'Art, Musée d'Art Moderne de la Ville de Paris, Paris 1978

Spot: Folk Art Environments, Houston Center of Photography, 1991

Straight At the Heart: Charles Smith's African/American Heritage Museum, Beloit College, Illinois, 1995

3. JOURNALS DEVOTED TO OUTSIDER ART:

GREAT BRITAIN:

Raw Vision

Raw Vision
163 Amsterdam Avenue, No 203
USA–New York, NY 10028-5001
Tel. +1-212-714 83 81
www.rawvision.com

1 Watford Road
Radlett
GB-Herts WD7 8LA
Tel. +44-(0)1923-85 66 44

37, rue de Gergovie
F-75014 Paris
Tel. +33-(0)1 40 44 96 46

International journal of intuitive and visionary art; Anglo-American production with news and reviews, featuring creations from all over the world.

Issues with particular reference to visionary environments:

Raw Vision #1:
Professor SS Bhatti: Nek Chand's Testament to Creativity
Seymour Rosen: The work of SPACES
John Maizels: French sites

Raw Vision #2:
John Turner: Howard Finster's Paradise Garden
Laurent Danchin: Chomo, the man whom death awaits

Raw Vision #3:
Bruno Montpied: The Garden of Charles Billy
John Maizels: The Art of Billy Morey
Barbara Brackman: Top Ten US Environments

Raw Vision #4:
George Melly: The Palais idéal of the Facteur Cheval
Verni Greenfield: Grandma Prisbrey's Bottle Village

Raw Vision #5:
Sue Ross: Helen Martins' Owl House
Jean-Claude Caire: Danielle Jacqui, She Who Paints

Raw Vision #6:
Bruno Montpied: The Bacchic Garden of Marcello Cammi
John Turner: The Buddha Park of Thailand
Phil Reeve: Learning Gardens of Thailand
Claude Arz: L'Eglise Verte de Réné Roualt

Raw Vision #7:
Jay Murphy: Lonnie Holley
Daro Montag: The Carved Rocks of Rothéneuf (Abbé Fouré)

Raw Vision #9:
Len Davidson : Errol McKenzie
Phil Reeve: Visit With the Master – Nek Chand
Kim Jenkins: Bodan Litnianski

Raw Vision #10:
John Clarke: Nukain Mabusa's Stone Garden

Raw Vision #11:
Paul Duechein: Nicolae Popa, Romanian carver
Jim Christy: Environments of British Columbia

Raw Vision #12:
Scott Wynn: Holy Land USA
Julia Duckett: The Watford Shell Garden

Raw Vision #13:
Claude Arz: Robert La Lagadec
Frédéric Allamel: Royal Robertson

Raw Vision #14:
Claude Arz: The Cathedral of Jean Linard

Raw Vision #15:
Dr Leo Navratil: Art & Psychiatry (Gugging)
Cynthia Alice Rubin: Margaret's Grocery

Raw Vision #16:
Larry Yust: Leonard Knight's Salvation Mountain

Raw Vision #19:
Dorothy Joiner: St EOM's Pasaquan

Raw Vision #20:
Jin Christy: Edward James' Jungle Paradise

Bib
liogr
aphy
Bibl
iogra
phie

Raw Vision #21:
  Kate Howlett Jones: Ben Wilson
  John MacGregor: Inner Architecture
  Ben Apfelbaum: Gordon's Patio

Raw Vision #22:
  Roberto Crocella: Bentivegna's Garden of
  Incantations

Raw Vision #23:
  Jim McCrary: Nativity Rock Museum

Raw Vision #24:
  John MacGregor: Tower of the Apocalypse
  (Eben-Ezer)

Raw Vision #25:
  Don Krug & Ann Perry Parker: Dr Evermor
  Marcus Schubert: Albino Carreira "Woodcakes"

Raw Vision #26:
  Debra Brehmer: Mary Nohl
  John Maizels: Jardin de la Luna Rossa

Raw Vision #27:
  Holly Metz: Palace Depression

FRANCE:

L'Œuf Sauvage
  www.oeufsauvage.com

  French quarterly publication, now out of print
  although still available.

  Issues with particular reference to visionary
  environments:

  L'Œuf Sauvage #3:
    Claude & Clovis Prévost: Raymond Isidore dit
    Picassiette

  L'Œuf Sauvage #7:
    Claude & Clovis Prévost: Robert Garcet et la Tour
    d'Apocalypse

  L'Œuf Sauvage #8:
    Jean-Louis Bédouin: Rothéneuf ou le génie du
    lieu (Abbé Fouré)

  L'Œuf Sauvage #9:
    Ferdinand Cheval, a letter to Monsieur Lepage

Bulletin les Amis d'Ozenda
  BP 44
  F–83690 Salernes
  Tel. +33–(0)4 94 70 60 66

  Voluminous newsletter of Les Amis, an
  organisation dedicated to the "artistes singuliers"
  of Southern France, which also contains news of
  events and environmental discoveries all over
  France. Available on subscription.

Création Franche
  58, avenue du Maréchal de Lattre de Tassigny
  F–33130 Bègles
  www.musee-creationfranche.com

  Magazine of the museum of the same name at
  Bègles. French text covering outsider artists in
  France.

Les Friches de l'Art
  Joe Ryczko
  2, impasse des Hortensias
  F–33500 Libourne

  Small French publication concentrating on
  Art Brut coverage.

Gazogène
  Jean-François Maurice
  108, rue Delpech
  F–46000 Cahors

  Small publication giving coverage to Outsider
  Art subjects in France.

SWITZERLAND:

Fascicules de l'Art Brut
  Collection de l'Art Brut
  Château de Beaulieu
  11, avenue de Bergières
  CH–1004 Lausanne
  Tel. +41–(0)21–647 54 35
  Fax +41–(0)21–648 55 21

  The official Art Brut publication from the
  Lausanne museum, originally designed and
  produced by Jean Dubuffet, gives in-depth
  coverage of artists in the Art Brut Collection;
  French text, extensive illustrations. Information
  on environments, exhibitions and publications.

  Issues with particular reference to visionary
  environments:

  Fascicule #9:
    A. Wolff: Il castello incantato de Filippo Bentivegna

  Fascicule #10:
    Bernard Chevassu: Louise Fisher

  Fascicule #11:
    Bernard Chevassu: François Portrat

  Fascicule #20:
    Pascal Sigoda: Camille Renault et le jardin des
    surprises
    Hans-Ulrich Schlumpf: La seconde vie d'Armand
    Schulthess

  Fascicule #20:
    Olivier Thiébaut: Auguste Le Boulche

USA:

Folk Art
  American Folk Art Museum
  45 West 53rd Street
  USA–New York, NY 10019
  Tel. +1–212–265 10 40
  www.folkartmuseum.org

  Official magazine of the Museum. Althoughly
  mainly concerned with American folk art,
  sometimes covers environments.

Folk Art Finder
  Gallery Press
  117 North Main Street
  USA–Essex, Connecticut 06426

  Fascinating small publication featuring new
  discoveries, opinion and debate. Some news of
  new environments. Available by subscription.

Folk Art Messenger
  P.O. Box 17041
  USA–Richmond, Virginia 23226
  www.folkart.org

  Organ of the Folk Art Society of America, gives
  news of FASA events and features exhibitions,
  reviews and debate. Available by subscription.

INTUIT
  756 North Milwaukee Avenue
  USA–Chicago, Illinois 60622
  Tel. +1–312–243 90 88
  www.art.org

  Newsletter of the organisation of the same
  name, it features news, reviews, and events.
  Available to members.

The Orange Press
  The Orange Show Foundation
  2402 Mungar Street
  USA–Houston, Texas 77023
  Tel. +1–713–926 63 68
  Fax +1–713–926 15 06
  www.orangeshow.org

  Newsletter of the Orange Show Foundation, it
  gives news of events, Art Car parades, and
  descriptions of local environments.

Index Register

The index lists all artists, visionary environments and places mentioned in the texts / Der Index führt alle Künstler, Visionary Environments und Orte auf, die in den Texten genannt werden / L'index mentionne tous les artistes, les environnements visionnaires et les places cités dans les textes